WITHDRAWN

Dogs 101: A Guide to American Kennel Club Breed Groups, Vol. 4 - The Terrier Group

Jacob Cleveland

Six Degrees Books. This book was created and put into distribution by a team of dedicated editors and subject matter experts using open source and proprietary publishing tools. The name "Six Degrees Books" is indicative of our desire to make it easy for people to find valuable, but not readily apparent, relationships between pieces of digital content and compile that information into helpful and interesting books.

Curation is King. One of the advantages to the way we publish books is that our content is up to date and written by dedicated subject matter experts from all over the world. By adding a layer of careful screening and curatorial attention to this, we are able to offer a book that is relevant, informative and unique.

We are looking to expand our team: If you are interested to be a Six Degrees editor and get paid for your subject matter expertise - please visit www.sixdegreesbooks.com.

Contents

Articles

Breed Groups (dog)	1
American Kennel Club	5
Terrier Group	11
Airedale Terrier	17
American Staffordshire Terrier	24
Australian Terrier	28
Bedlington Terrier	30
Border Terrier	33
Bull Terrier	36
Cairn Terrier	41
Dandie Dinmont Terrier	48
Glen of Imaal Terrier	50
Irish Terrier	51
Kerry Blue Terrier	56
Lakeland Terrier	59
Manchester Terrier	61
Bull Terrier (Miniature)	64
Miniature Schnauzer	67
Norfolk Terrier	72
Norwich Terrier	75
Parson Russell Terrier	78
Scottish Terrier	81
Sealyham Terrier	88
Skye Terrier	90
Fox Terrier (Smooth)	92
Soft-Coated Wheaten Terrier	95

Staffordshire Bull Terrier   97

Welsh Terrier   102

West Highland White Terrier   104

Wire Fox Terrier   107

References

Article Sources and Contributors   111

Breed Groups (dog)

A **Breed Group** is a categorization of related breeds of animal by an overseeing organization, used to organize the showing of animals. In dogs, kennel clubs define the *Breed Groups* and decide which dog breeds are to be included in each *Breed Group*. The Fédération Cynologique Internationale *Breed Groups* are used to organize dogs for international competition. *Breed Groups* often have the names of, and are loosely based on, ancestral dog types of modern dog breeds.

Recognized Breed Groups

International

The Fédération Cynologique Internationale makes sure that dogs in its 84 member countries can compete together, by establishing common nomenclature and making sure that pedigrees are mutually recognized in all the member countries. So internationally, dog breeds are organized in ten groups, each with subsections according to breed type and origin.

- **Group 1 - Sheepdogs and Cattle Dogs (except Swiss Cattle Dogs)**
- **Group 2 Pinscher and Schnauzer - Molossoid Breeds - Swiss Mountain and Cattle Dogs**
  - Section 1: Pinscher and Schnauzer type
  - Section 2: Molossoid breeds
  - Section 3: Swiss Mountain and Cattle Dogs
- **Group 3 Terriers**
  - Section 1: Large and medium-sized Terriers
  - Section 2: Small-sized Terriers
  - Section 3: Bull type Terriers
  - Section 4: Toy Terriers
- **Group 4 Dachshunds**
- **Group 5 Spitz and Primitive types**
  - Section 1: Nordic Sledge Dogs
  - Section 2: Nordic Hunting Dogs
  - Section 3: Nordic Watchdogs and Herders
  - Section 4: European Spitz
  - Section 5: Asian Spitz and related breeds
  - Section 6: Primitive type
  - Section 7: Primitive type - Hunting Dogs
  - Section 8: Primitive type Hunting Dogs with a ridge on the back

- **Group 6 Scenthounds and Related Breeds**
  - Section 1: Scenthounds
  - Section 2: Leash (scent) Hounds
  - Section 3: Related breeds (Dalmatian and Rhodesian Ridgeback)
- **Group 7 Pointing Dogs**
  - Section 1: Continental Pointing Dogs
  - Section 2: British and Irish Pointers and Setters
- **Group 8 Retrievers - Flushing Dogs - Water Dogs**
  - Section 1: Retrievers
  - Section 2: Flushing Dogs
  - Section 3: Water Dogs
- **Group 9 Companion and Toy Dogs**
  - Section 1: Bichons and related breeds
  - Section 2: Poodle
  - Section 3: Small Belgian Dogs
  - Section 4: Hairless Dogs
  - Section 5: Tibetan breeds
  - Section 6: Chihuahueñ o
  - Section 7: English Toy Spaniels
  - Section 8: Japan Chin and Pekingese
  - Section 9: Continental Toy Spaniel
  - Section 10: Kromfohrländer
  - Section 11: Small Molossian type Dogs
- **Group 10 Sighthounds**
  - Section 1: Long-haired or fringed Sighthounds
  - Section 2: Rough-haired Sighthounds
  - Section 3: Short-haired Sighthounds

The Kennel Club

The Kennel Club (UK) is the original and oldest kennel club; it is not a member of the Fédération Cynologique Internationale. For The Kennel Club, dogs are placed in the following groups:

- Hound Group
- Gundog Group
- Terrier Group
- Utility Group
- Working Group

- Pastoral Group
- Toy Group

Working is here meant to indicate dogs that are not hunting dogs that work directly for people, such as police dogs, search and rescue dogs, and others. It does not imply that other types of dogs do not work. Dogs that work with livestock are in the Pastoral Group.

Australia and New Zealand

The Australian National Kennel Council and the New Zealand Kennel Club recognize similar groups to The Kennel Club.

Australian National Kennel Council recognized Breed Groups:

- Group 1 (Toys)
- Group 2 (Terriers)
- Group 3 (Gundogs)
- Group 4 (Hounds)
- Group 5 (Working Dogs)
- Group 6 (Utility)
- Group 7 (Non Sporting)

New Zealand Kennel Club recognized Breed Groups:

- Toy Group
- Terrier Group
- Gundogs
- Hound Group
- Working Group
- Utility Group
- Non Sporting Group

North America

The Canadian Kennel Club and the two major kennel clubs in the United States have similar groups, although they may not include the same dogs in the same groupings. Canadian Kennel Club recognized Breed Groups:

- Group 1, Sporting Dogs
- Group 2, Hounds
- Group 3, Working Dogs
- Group 4, Terriers
- Group 5, Toys
- Group 6, Non-Sporting
- Group 7, Herding

American Kennel Club recognized Breed Groups:

- Sporting Group
- Hound Group
- Working Group
- Terrier Group
- Toy Group
- Non-Sporting Group
- Herding Group

United Kennel Club (US) recognized Breed Groups:

- Companion Dog Group
- Guardian Dog Group
- Gun Dog Group
- Herding Dog Group
- Northern Breed Group
- Scenthound Group
- Sighthound & Pariah Group
- Terrier Group

Other

The major national kennel club for each country will organize breeds in breed groups. The naming and organization of *Breed Groups* may vary from country to country. In addition, some rare new breeds or newly documented traditional breeds may be awaiting approval by a given kennel club, and may not yet be assigned to a particular *Breed Group*.

In addition to the major registries, there are a nearly infinite number of sporting clubs, breed clubs, minor kennel clubs, and internet-based breed registries and dog registration businesses in which breeds may be organized into whatever Breed Group the club, minor registry, or dog business may devise.

See also

- Dog type
- Dog breed
- Conformation show
- General Specials

External links

- http://www.dogsonline.com
- http://www.dogsindepth.com/index.html Dog Breed Groups from dogsindepth.com the online dog encyclopedia
- http://www.u-c-i.de/

American Kennel Club

The **American Kennel Club** (or **AKC**) is a registry of purebred dog pedigrees in the United States. Beyond maintaining its pedigree registry, this kennel club also promotes and sanctions events for purebred dogs, including the Westminster Kennel Club Dog Show, an annual event which predates the official forming of the AKC, the National Dog Show, and the AKC/Eukanuba National Championship. Unlike most other country's kennels clubs, the AKC is not part of the Fédération Cynologique Internationale (World Canine Organization).

Dog registration

The AKC is not the only registry of purebred dogs, but it is the only non-profit registry and the one with which most Americans are familiar. Founded in 1884, the AKC is the largest purebred dog registry in the world. Along with its nearly 5,000 licensed and member clubs and affiliated organizations, the AKC advocates for the purebred dog as a family companion, advances canine health and well-being, works to protect the rights of all dog owners and promotes responsible dog ownership. An example of dogs registered elsewhere in the U.S. is the National Greyhound Association which registers racing greyhounds (which are legally not considered "pets").

For a purebred dog to be registered with the AKC, the dog's parents must be registered with the AKC as the same breed, and the litter in which the dog is born must be registered with the AKC. If the dog's parents are not registered with the AKC or the litter is not registered, special registry research by the AKC is necessary for the AKC to determine if the dog is eligible for AKC registration. Once a determination of eligibility is met, either by litter application or registry research, the dog can be registered as purebred by the AKC.To register a mixed breed dog with AKC as a Canine Partner, you may go to the AKC website and enroll the dog via an online form. Once registered, your mixed breed dog will be eligible to compete in the AKC Agility, Obedience and AKC Rally® Events. 2010 Most Popular Dogs in the U.S.

1. Labrador Retriever

2. German Shepherd Dog

3. Yorkshire Terrier

4. Golden Retriever

5. Beagle

6. Boxer

7. Bulldog

8. Dachshund

9. Poodle

10. Shih Tzu

Registration indicates only that the dog's parents were registered as one recognized breed; it does not necessarily indicate that the dog comes from healthy or show-quality blood lines. Nor is registration necessarily a reflection on the quality of the breeder or how the puppy was raised. Registration is necessary only for breeders (so they can sell registered puppies) or for purebred conformation show or purebred dog sports participation. Registration can be obtained by mail or online at their website.

AKC and health

Even though the AKC supports some canine health research and has run advertising campaigns implying that the AKC is committed to healthy dogs, the AKC's role in furthering dog health is controversial. Temple Grandin maintains that the AKC's standards only regulate physical appearance, not emotional or behavioral health. The AKC has no health standards for breeding. The only breeding restriction is age (a dog can be no younger than 8 months.) Furthermore, the AKC prohibits clubs from imposing stricter regulations, that is, an AKC breed club cannot require a higher breeding age, hip dysplasia ratings, genetic tests for inheritable diseases, or any other restrictions. Parent clubs do have the power to define the looks of the breed, or breed standard. Parent club may also restrict participation in non-regular events or classes such as Futurities or Maturities to only those dogs meeting their defined criteria. This enables those non-regular events to require health testing, DNA sampling, instinct/ability testing and other outlined requirements as established by the hosting club of the non-regular event.

As a result, attention to health among breeders is purely voluntary. By contrast, many dog clubs outside the US do require health tests of breeding dogs. The German Shepherd Club of Germany [1], for example, requires hip and elbow X-rays in addition to other tests before a dog can be bred. Such breeding restrictions are not allowed in AKC member clubs. As a result, some US breeders have established parallel registries or health databases outside of the AKC; for example, the Berner Garde [2] established such a database in 1995 after genetic diseases reduced the average lifespan of a Bernese Mountain Dog to 7 years. The Swiss Bernese Mountain Dog club introduced mandatory hip X-rays in 1971.

For these, and other reasons, a small number of breed clubs have not yet joined the AKC so they can maintain stringent health standards, but, in general, the breeders' desire to show their dogs at AKC shows such as the Westminster Dog Show has won out over these concerns.

Contrary to most western nations organized under the International Kennel Federation (of which the AKC is not a member), the AKC has not removed docked tails and cropped ears from the requirements of many AKC breed standards, even though this practice is opposed in the U.S. by the American Veterinary Medical Association, and banned by law in many other countries.

The Club has also been criticized for courting large scale commercial breeders.

Purebred Alternative Listing Program / Indefinite Listing Privilege Program

The Purebred Alternative Listing Program (PAL), formerly the Indefinite Listing Privilege Program (ILP), is an AKC program that provides purebred dogs who may not have been eligible for registration a chance to register "alternatively" (formerly "indefinitely"). There are various reasons why a purebred dog might not be eligible for registration; for example, the dog may be the product of an unregisterable litter, or have unregisterable parents. Many dogs enrolled in the PAL and ILP programs were adopted from animal shelters or rescue groups, in which case the status of the dog's parents is unknown. Dogs enrolled in PAL/ILP may participate in AKC companion and performance activities, but not conformation. Enrollees of the program receive various benefits, including a subscription to *Family Dog* Magazine, a certificate for their dog's place in the PAL, and information about AKC Pet Healthcare and microchipping. Dogs that were registered under the ILP program keep their original numbers.

AKC National Championship

The AKC/Eukanuba National Championship is an annual event held in both Tampa, FL, and Long Beach, CA. The show is by invitation only. The dogs invited to the show have either finished their championship from the bred-by-exhibitor class or ranked in the Top 25 of their breed. The show can often be seen on major television stations.

Open foundation stock

The Foundation Stock Service (FSS) is an AKC program for breeds not yet accepted by the AKC for full recognition, and not yet in the AKC's Miscellaneous class. The AKC FSS requires that at least the parents of the registered animal are known. The AKC will not grant championship points to dogs in these breeds until the stud book is closed and the breed is granted full recognition.

Activities

The AKC sanctions events in which dogs and handlers can compete. These are divided into three areas:

- Conformation shows
  - Junior Showmanship
- Companion events, in which all registered and PAL/ILP dogs can compete. These include:
  - Obedience trials
  - Tracking trials
  - Dog agility
  - Rally obedience
- Performance events, which are limited to certain entrants; PAL/ILP dogs of the correct breed are usually eligible:
  - Coonhound events (coonhounds; no PAL/ILP dogs)
  - Field trials (hounds)
  - Earthdog trials (small terriers and Dachshunds)
  - Sheepdog trials (herding tests) (herding breeds, Rottweilers, and Samoyeds)
  - Hunt tests (most dogs in the Sporting Groups and Standard Poodles)
  - Lure coursing (sighthounds only)
  - Working Dog Sport (obedience, tracking, protection) German Shepherds, Doberman Pinschers, Rottweilers, Bouvier des Flandres

AKC policy toward working dog sport events that include protection phases, such as Schutzhund, has changed according to prevailing public sentiment in the United States. In 1990, as well-publicized dog attacks were driving public fear against many breeds, the AKC issued a ban on protection sports for all of its member clubs. After the terrorist attacks of 9/11/2001, Americans began to take a more positive attitude toward well-trained protection dogs, and in July 2003 the AKC decided to allow member clubs to hold a limited number of protection events with prior written permission. In 2006 the AKC released rules for its own Working Dog Sport events, very similar to Schutzhund.

In 2007, the American Kennel Club accepted an invitation from the Mexican Kennel Club to participate in the Fédération Cynologique Internationale World Dog Show in Mexico City.

Recognized breeds

As of July 2009, the AKC fully recognizes 163 breeds with 12 additional breeds granted partial status in the Miscellaneous class. Another 62 rare breeds can be registered in its Foundation Stock Service.

The AKC divides dog breeds into seven *groups*, one *class*, and the Foundation Stock Service, consisting of the following (as of July 2009):

- Sporting Group: 28 breeds developed as bird dogs. Includes Pointers, Retrievers, Setters, and Spaniels.
- Hound Group: 25 breeds developed to hunt using sight (sighthounds) or scent (scent hounds). Includes Greyhounds and Beagles.
- Working Group: 26 large breeds developed for a variety of jobs, including guarding property, guarding livestock, or pulling carts. Includes Siberian Huskies and Bernese Mountain Dogs.
- Terrier Group: 27 feisty breeds some of which were developed to hunt vermin and to dig them from their burrows or lairs. Size ranges from the tiny Cairn Terrier to the large Airedale Terrier.
- Toy Group: 21 small companion breeds Includes Toy Poodles and Pekineses.
- Non-Sporting Group: 17 breeds that do not fit into any of the preceding categories, usually larger than Toy dogs. Includes Bichon Frises and Miniature Poodles.
- Herding Group: 22 breeds developed to herd livestock. Includes Rough Collies and Belgian Shepherds.
- Best in Show:over 150 breeds All Breeds
- Miscellaneous Class: 11 breeds that have advanced from FSS but that are not yet fully recognized. After a period of time that ensures that good breeding practices are in effect and that the gene pool for the breed is ample, the breed is moved to one of the seven preceding groups.
- Foundation Stock Service (FSS) Program: 62 breeds. This is a breed registry in which breeders of rare breeds can record the birth and parentage of a breed that they are trying to establish in the United States; these dogs provide the *foundation stock* from which eventually a fully recognized breed might result. These breeds cannot participate in AKC events until at least 150 individual dogs are registered; thereafter, competition in various events is then provisional.

The AKC Board of Directors appointed a committee in October, 2007, to evaluate the current alignment of breeds within the seven variety groups. Reasons for the action included the growing number of breeds in certain groups, and the make-up of breeds within certain groups. The number of groups and group make-up has been modified in the past, providing precedent for this action. The Group Realignment Committee completed their report in July, 2008.

The committee recommended that the seven variety groups be replaced with ten variety groups. If this proposal is approved, the Hound Group would be divided into "Scent Hounds" and "Sight Hounds"; the Sporting Group would be divided into "Sporting Group – Pointers and Setters" and "Sporting Group –

Retrievers and Spaniels"; a new group called the "Northern Group" would be created; and the Non-Sporting Group would be renamed the "Companion Group". The Northern Group would be populated by Northern/Spitz breeds, consisting of the Norwegian Elkhound, Akita, Alaskan Malamute, Siberian Husky, Samoyed, American Eskimo, Chinese Shar-Pei, Chow Chow, Finnish Spitz, Keeshond, Schipperke, Shiba Inu and Swedish Vallhund. In addition, the Italian Greyhound is proposed to be moved to the Sight Hound Group, and the Dalmatian is proposed to be moved to the Working Group.

See also: American Kennel Club Groups

Other AKC programs

The AKC also offers the Canine Good Citizen program. This program tests dogs of any breed (including mixed breed) or type, registered or not, for basic behavior and temperament suitable for appearing in public and living at home.

The AKC also supports Canine Health with the Canine Health Foundation http://www.akcchf.org/

Another AKC affiliate is AKC Companion Animal Recovery (AKC CAR), the nation's largest not-for-profit pet identification and 24/7 recovery service provider. AKC CAR is a leading distributor of pet microchips in the U.S. and a participant in AAHA's free Pet Microchip Lookup tool.

AKC and legislation

The AKC tracks all dog related legislation in the United States, lobbies lawmakers and issues legislative alerts on the internet asking for citizens to contact public officials. They are particularly active in combating breed-specific legislation such as bans on certain breeds considered dangerous. They also combat most legislation to protect animals such as breed-limit restrictions and anti-puppy mill legislation. While they argue that their motive is to protect legitimate breeders and the industry, many argue their incentive is purely financial.

See also

- List of dog breeds
- United Kennel Club
- DOGNY
- American Dog Club
- World Wide Kennel Club
- List of Kennel Clubs by Country

External links

- Official website [3]
- AKC CAR's Official website [4]
- 2007 Registration Data [5]
- The Politics of Dogs: Criticism of Policies of AKC [6] The Atlantic, 1990
- Digging into the AKC: Taking cash for tainted dogs [7] The Philadelphia Inquirer, 1995
- Doogle.Info Worldwide online dog database and pedigree [8]

Terrier Group

Terrier Group is the name of a breed Group of dogs, used by kennel clubs to classify a defined collection of dog breeds. In general, a *Terrier Group* includes one particular type of dog, the Terrier, although other types may be included in a kennel club's *Terrier Group*. Most major English-language kennel clubs include a *Terrier Group* although different kennel clubs may not include the same breeds in their *Terrier Group*. The international kennel club association, the Fédération Cynologique Internationale, includes Terriers in Group 3 *Terrier*, which is then further broken down into four *Sections* based on the type of terrier and breed history.

Terrier dogs

Terrier-type dogs were originally kept to hunt vermin, especially mice and rats. Some were small enough to go down the holes of the European fox and other agricultural pest animals in order to chase them out for the hunter, and the name *terrier* is from the Latin *terra*, meaning earth, in reference to the dogs going underground. Today, the majority of modern breeds developed from the old terrier types are pets and companions. A few are still used as working terriers, and some terriers are large enough to be kept as guard dogs.

Terrier Group breeds

Kennel clubs assign breeds traditionally identified as terriers to their *Terrier Group*. Some kennel clubs prefer to use another category such as the Toy Group, Companion Group, Utility Group or Non-Sporting Group for certain terriers or terrier-like breeds, but most terriers are placed in the *Terrier Group*.

The United Kennel Club (US) is unusual in that it recognises Pinschers and Feists in its *Terrier Group*, along with other US breeds not recognised elsewhere. The United Kennel Club also lists the Hollandse Smoushond with the Terriers, which it resembles, but is elsewhere considered a Schnauzer-type breed. Another Schnauzer, the miniature Schnauzer (or Zwergschnauzer), is sometimes placed in a kennel club's *Terrier Group*. The Boston Terrier is usually listed by kennel clubs in the *Companion Group* or the *Non-Sporting Group*.

The American Kennel Club does recognize the Russell Terrier, although currently the breed is listed within the Foundation Stock Service (FSS) which is not categorized into the Terrier group. Additionally, the United Kennel Club (UKC)changed the classifications of the different types of Russells starting in 2009. The Jack Russell Terrier prior to this time was really a Parson Russell Terrier (by AKC's standards) with an over 12" and under 12" breed types offered. The traditional Parson Russell Terriers were classified within the over 12" category while the traditional Jack Russell Terriers were classified within the under 12" category. The Russell Terrier, prior to 2009, included the shorter legged and longer backed variations of the breed. When the classifications were changed, the dogs within the Jack Russell Terrier breed that were over 12" tall at the withers were moved into the Parson Russell Terrier breed. Any dog in the Jack Russell Terrier breed at this time (within the UKC) may not be over 12" tall. The Russell Terrier breed has been blended into the Jack Russell Terrier breed within the UKC.

Comparison of Terrier Group breeds of major kennel clubs

Terrier Group breeds of major kennel clubs

The Kennel Club (UK) Terrier Group	Canadian Kennel Club Terrier Dogs Group	American Kennel Club Terrier Group	Australian National Kennel Council Terrier Dogs Group	New Zealand Kennel Club Terrier Group	United Kennel Club (US) Terrier Group
Airedale Terrier	Airedale Terrier	Airedale Terrier	Airedale Terrier	Airedale Terrier	Airedale Terrier
Australian Terrier	American Staffordshire Terrier	American Staffordshire Terrier	American Staffordshire Terrier	American Staffordshire Terrier	American Hairless Terrier
Bedlington Terrier	Australian Terrier	Australian Terrier	Australian Terrier	Australian Terrier	American Pit Bull Terrier
Border Terrier	Bedlington Terrier	Bedlington Terrier	Bedlington Terrier	Bedlington Terrier	Australian Terrier
Bull Terrier	Border Terrier	Border Terrier	Border Terrier	Border Terrier	Austrian Pinscher
Bull Terrier (Miniature)	Bull Terrier	Bull Terrier	Bull Terrier	Bull Terrier	Bedlington Terrier
Cairn Terrier	Bull Terrier (Miniature)	Cairn Terrier	Bull Terrier (Miniature)	Bull Terrier (Miniature)	Border Terrier
Cesky Terrier	Cairn Terrier	Dandie Dinmont Terrier	Cairn Terrier	Cairn Terrier	Bull Terrier
Dandie Dinmont Terrier	Cesky Terrier	Glen of Imaal Terrier	Cesky Terrier	Cesky Terrier	Cairn Terrier

Fox Terrier (Smooth)	Dandie Dinmont Terrier	Irish Terrier	Dandie Dinmont Terrier	Dandie Dinmont Terrier	Cesky Terrier
Fox Terrier (Wire)	Fox Terrier (Smooth)	Kerry Blue Terrier	Fox Terrier (Smooth)	Fox Terrier (Smooth)	Dandie Dinmont Terrier
Glen of Imaal Terrier	Fox Terrier (Wire)	Lakeland Terrier	Fox Terrier (Wire)	Fox Terrier (Wire)	Dutch Smoushond
Irish Terrier	Irish Terrier	Manchester Terrier	German Hunting Terrier	German Hunting Terrier	German Pinscher
Kerry Blue Terrier	Kerry Blue Terrier	Miniature Bull Terrier	Glen Of Imaal Terrier	Glen Of Imaal Terrier	Glen of Imaal Terrier
Lakeland Terrier	Lakeland Terrier	Miniature Schnauzer	Irish Terrier	Irish Terrier	Irish Terrier
Manchester Terrier	Manchester Terrier	Norfolk Terrier	Jack Russell Terrier	Jack Russell Terrier	Jagdterrier
Norfolk Terrier	Norfolk Terrier	Norwich Terrier	Kerry Blue Terrier	Kerry Blue Terrier	Japanese Terrier
Norwich Terrier	Norwich Terrier	Parson Russell Terrier	Lakeland Terrier	Lakeland Terrier	Kerry Blue Terrier
Parson Russell Terrier	Parson Russell Terrier	Scottish Terrier	Manchester Terrier	Manchester Terrier	Kromfohrlander
Scottish Terrier	Schnauzer (Miniature)	Sealyham Terrier	Norfolk-Terrier	Norfolk Terrier	Lakeland Terrier
Sealyham Terrier	Scottish Terrier	Skye Terrier	Norwich Terrier	Norwich Terrier	Manchester Terrier
Skye Terrier	Sealyham Terrier	Smooth Fox Terrier	Parson Russell Terrier	Parson Russell Terrier	Miniature Bull Terrier
Soft Coated Wheaten Terrier	Skye Terrier	Soft Coated Wheaten Terrier	Scottish Terrier	Scottish Terrier	Miniature Schnauzer
Staffordshire Bull Terrier	Soft-Coated Wheaten Terrier	Staffordshire Bull Terrier	Sealyham Terrier	Sealyham Terrier	Norfolk Terrier
Welsh Terrier	Staffordshire Bull Terrier	Welsh Terrier	Skye Terrier	Skye Terrier	Norwich Terrier
West Highland White Terrier	Welsh Terrier	West Highland White Terrier	Soft Coated Wheaten Terrier	Soft Coated Wheaten Terrier	Parson Russell Terrier
	West Highland White Terrier	Wire Fox Terrier	Staffordshire Bull Terrier	Staffordshire Bull Terrier	Jack Russell Terrier
			Tenterfield Terrier	Tenterfield Terrier	Patterdale Terrier
			Welsh Terrier	Welsh Terrier	Rat Terrier

			West Highland White Terrier	West Highland White Terrier	Russell Terrier
					Scottish Terrier
					Sealyham Terrier
					Silky Terrier
					Skye Terrier
					Smooth Fox Terrier
					Soft-Coated Wheaten Terrier
					Sporting Lucas Terrier
					Staffordshire Bull Terrier
					Teddy Roosevelt Terrier
					Toy Fox Terrier
					Treeing Feist
					Welsh Terrier
					West Highland White Terrier
					Wire Fox Terrier

Terriers by Fédération Cynologique Internationale Sections

The Fédération Cynologique Internationale breaks down their Terrier and Companion Group (Group 3) into *Sections* by general dog type; within the sections the dogs are listed by their country or area of origin. Also included in the Sections are variants and colours that have to do with how they are organised during dog shows.

Fédération Cynologique Internationale recognised Terrier breeds are sorted into four sections, shown below (with their identification number.)

Fédération Cynologique Internationale Terrier breeds by Section

Section 1: Large and medium-sized Terriers

341 Brazilian Terrier (Terrier Brasileiro)	103 Deutscher Jagdterrier	7 Airedale Terrier
9 Bedlington Terrier	10 Border Terrier	12 Fox Terrier (Smooth)
169 Fox Terrier (Wire)	70 Lakeland Terrier	71 Manchester Terrier
339 Parson Russell Terrier	78 Welsh Terrier	302 Irish Glen of Imaal Terrier
139 Irish Terrier	3 Kerry Blue Terrier	40 Irish Soft Coated Wheaten Terrier

Section 2: Small-sized Terriers

8 Australian Terrier	345 Jack Russell Terrier	4 Cairn Terrier
168 Dandie Dinmont Terrier	272 Norfolk Terrier	72 Norwich Terrier
73 Scottish Terrier	74 Sealyham Terrier	75 Skye Terrier
85 West Highland White Terrier	259 Nihon Teria (Japanese Terrier)	246 Cesky Terrier

Section 3: Bull-type Terriers

Bull Terrier (11) a) Bull Terrier (Standard)	Bull Terrier (11) b) Bull Terrier (Miniature)	76 Staffordshire Bull Terrier
286 American Staffordshire Terrier		

Section 4: Toy Terriers

236 Australian Silky Terrier	13 English Toy Terrier (Black and Tan)	86 Yorkshire Terrier
Russkiy Toy (provisional)		

Photographs of other terriers, not Fédération Cynologique Internationale recognised, provisionally recognised, or recognised in some Fédération Cynologique Internationale Group other than Terrier are shown below:

Schnauzer (Miniature) placed in the Terrier Group by many kennel clubs	Tenterfield Terrier	American Pit Bull Terrier
American Hairless Terrier	Dutch Smoushond (Group 2, Schnauzer)	Patterdale Terrier
Rat Terrier	Russell Terrier	Teddy Roosevelt Terrier
Russian Black Terrier	Australian Silky Terrier	Boston Terrier
Miniature Fox Terrier	Toy Manchester Terrier	Tibetan Terrier
Toy Fox Terrier	Austrian Pinscher	

Other clubs

Most kennel clubs in non-English speaking countries include a *Terrier Group.*

Terriers are also included in the listings of the enormous and ever-expanding number of specialty registries, minor kennel clubs, dog sports clubs, breed clubs, rare dog registries, and internet based dog clubs and businesses. Each will have its own definition of what breeds belong in their own Terrier Group.

Terriers, especially the smaller breeds, have been used for crossbreeding to create what are called designer dogs, bred either accidentally or to enhance the marketability of puppies, often with cute portmanteau names created from syllables of each breed name. Although there are clubs willing to "register" such designer dogs, they are not breeds of dog. Breeders may call designer dogs *terriers* but they are not part of the *Terrier Group* of any major kennel club.

The Jack Russell Terrier is notable in that its primary breed club, the Jack Russell Terrier Club of America, specifically regulates inbreeding and linebreeding to a 16% coefficient of relationship. However, it is still a modern purebred dog breed, descended from known ancestors, and crossbred (with another breed of dog) dogs are not registerable.

See also

- Breed Groups (dog)
- Terrier
- Pet
- Working terrier
- Companion dog
- Companion Group

Airedale Terrier

The **Airedale Terrier** (often shortened to "Airedale") is a breed of the terrier type, originating in Airedale, a geographic area in Yorkshire, England. It is traditionally called the "King of Terriers" because it is the largest of the terrier breeds. Having been bred from a Welsh Terrier and an Otter Hound, the breed has also been called the **Waterside Terrier**, because it was bred originally to hunt otters in and around the valleys of the River Aire which runs through Airedale. In England this breed has also been used as a police dog.

Description

Appearance

The Airedale is the largest of the Terriers originating in Britain. They weigh and have a height at the withers of for dogs, with females slightly smaller. The American Kennel Club standard specifies a smaller dog. Larger ADTs, up to can be found in the New World. They are often called "Oorangs." This was the name of a kennel in Ohio in the early 1900s.

The Airedale has a medium length black and tan coat with a harsh topcoat and a soft undercoat. They are an alert and energetic breed, "not aggressive but fearless." It has been claimed that the large "hunting" type or Oorang airedales are more game than the smaller "show" type airedales. The large type are usually used for big game hunting and as family guardians or as pets, but usually do poorly in AKC conformation shows.The airedale terrier is the second largest of the terriers and stands square in appearance, with the largest being the Black Russian terrier.

Coat

Like many terriers, the breed has a 'broken' coat. The coat is hard, dense and wiry, not so long as to appear ragged, and lies straight and close, covering body and legs. The outer coat is hard, wiry and stiff, while the undercoat shorter and softer. The hardest coats are crinkling or just slightly waved. Curly soft coats are highly undesirable.

Airedales being shown or those who want their Airedale's coat to look healthy are generally groomed by *hand stripping* where a small serrated edged knife is used to pull out loose hair from the dog's coat. With regular grooming, the Airedale may shed very little. Although the Airedale often appears on lists of dogs that do not shed (moult), this is misleading. Every hair in the dog coat grows from a hair follicle, and has a cycle of growing, then being shed, then being replaced by another hair in the same follicle. The length of time of the growing and shedding cycle varies by breed, age, and by whether the dog is an inside or outside dog. It may be that "there is no such thing as a nonshedding breed."

The "correct" (according to the AKC breed standard) coat color is either a black saddle, with a tan head, ears and legs; or a dark grizzle saddle (black mixed with gray and white).

Tail

The Airedale's tail is usually docked (surgically shortened) within five days of birth, but this is not a requirement of breed standard authorities. To show an Airedale in the United States, the official AKC standard states "The root of the tail should be set well up on the back. It should be carried gaily but not curled over the back. It should be of good strength and substance and of fair length"., while in the UK it is illegal to dock dogs' tails unless it is for the dog's benefit (e.g., if the tail is broken). Traditionally the fluffy tail is left long.

Eyes

The Airedale's eyes "should be dark in colour, small, not prominent, full of terrier expression, keenness and intelligence" Light or bold eyes are considered highly undesirable.

Some Airedales do suffer from eye diseases, such as congenital retina conditions.

Mouth

Airedales have a normal 'scissor bite', where the top teeth close over the bottom. The Airedale's teeth were developed in this way so he could defend himself against quarry he was originally bred to chase.

Size

Airedale terrier males should measure approximately 24 inches in height at the shoulder; bitches, slightly less. There is no mention of a specific weight, although the standard states that both sexes should be sturdy, well muscled and boned. At 23 to 24 inches, a dog should weigh approximately 50 - 70 pounds, being active and agile enough to perform well, while not too small to function as a physical deterrent, retriever or hunter. Some breeders have produced larger Airedale Terriers, such as the 'Oorang Airedale', developed in the 1920s.

Ex-Army captain and Airdale breeder Walter Lingo's monthly magazine "Oorang Comments" (#25, page 81), stated unequivocally that "When full grown your Airedale dog will weigh from forty to fifty-five pounds and if a female will weigh slightly less. This is the standard weight, but when required, we can furnish over-sized Airedales whose weight will be from sixty to one hundred pounds."

Because Lingo tried to fill orders for everyone, the Oorang strain size was never standardized. Airedales weighing from 40 to 100 pounds were produced, but for the most part they were approximately 50 pounds and 22 to 24 inches at the shoulder.

Temperament

The Airedale can be used as a working dog and also as a hunting dog. Airedales exhibit some herding characteristics as well, and have a propensity to chase animals. They have no problem working with cattle and livestock. However, an Airedale that is not well trained will agitate and annoy the animals. Strong-willed, with the tenacity commonly seen in terriers, the Airedale is a formidable opponent.

The Airedale Terrier, like most Terriers, has been bred to hunt independently. As a result, the dog is very intelligent, independent, strong-minded, stoic, and can sometimes be stubborn. They rank 29th in Stanley Coren's The Intelligence of Dogs, being of above average working/obedience intelligence. The Airedale is a dog with a great sense of humor. For those who can laugh along with their Airedale, the dog can provide a unique and entertaining company. For those who don't appreciate being outsmarted by their dog, owning an Airedale can be a trying experience. Patience and consistency in training will be rewarded as the Airedales have been known to reach great heights in competitive obedience, dog agility, and Schutzhund. Airedales need an owner that can be creative in teaching what is expected. Airedales usually get bored easily and need a trainer that has the ability to make working fun and exciting. Changing the routine or taking a play-break is much more productive than trying to force the Airedale. If children and Airedale are both trained correctly, Airedales can be an excellent choice for a family dog.

Albert Payson Terhune wrote of the Airedale: "Among the mine-pits of the Aire, the various groups of miners each sought to develop a dog which could outfight and outhunt and outthink the other miner's dogs. Tests of the first-named virtues were made in inter-mine dog fights. Bit by bit, thus, an active, strong, heroic, compactly graceful and clever dog was evolved – the earliest true form of the Airedale.

He is swift, formidable, graceful, big of brain, an ideal chum and guard. ....To his master he is an adoring pal. To marauders he is a destructive lightning bolt."

They are also very loving, always in the middle of the family activities. Airedales are also known for expressing exactly what they are thinking, unlike more aloof breeds. The Airedale is also a reliable and protective family pet. Airedales are exceedingly loyal and strong dogs; there is one story of an Airedale taking down a bear to protect its master. They are very energetic, and need plenty of exercise.

The Airedale is also stoic, able to withstand pain and injury. An Airedale's injuries and illnesses often go unnoticed until they become severe and require veterinary attention.The airedale terrier will usually do ok with children if they have early exposure and socialization, however they may play too rough for very small ones.

Health

Mortality

Airedale Terriers in UK, USA, and Canadian surveys had a median lifespan of about 11.5 years, which is similar to other breeds of their size.

In a 2004 UK Kennel Club survey, the most common causes of death were cancer (39.5%), old age (14%), urologic (9%), and cardiac (7%) . In a 2000–2001 USA/Canada Health Survey, the most common causes of death were cancer (38%), urologic (17%), old age (12%), and cardiac (6%).A very hardy breed,although some may suffer from eye problems,hip dysplasia and skin infections.

Morbidity

Airedales can be affected by hip dysplasia.

Like most terriers, they have a propensity towards dermatitis. Skin disorders may go unnoticed in Airedales, because of their hard, dense, wiry coats. Itchy skin may be manifest as acral lick dermatitis (caused by licking one area excessively) or acute moist dermatitis or "hot spots" (an oppressively itchy, inflamed and oozing patch of skin, made worse by intense licking and chewing). Allergies, dietary imbalances, and under/over-productive thyroid glands are the main causes of skin conditions.

An Airedale's coat was originally designed to protect the dog from its predators--the coat was designed to come out in the claws of the predator the dog was designed to hunt, leaving the dog unharmed. Because of this, some forms of skin dermatitis can respond to hand stripping the coat. Clipping the coat cuts the dead hair, leaving dead roots within the hair follicles. It is these dead roots which can cause skin irritations. However, hand stripping removes these dead roots from the skin and stimulates new growth. Hence this process can assist with some forms of skin irritations.

Gastric torsion, or bloat, affects Airedale Terriers. Bloat can turn and block the stomach, causing a buildup of gas. Bloat can be fatal, it can lead to cardiovascular collapse. Signs of bloat are gastric distress (stomach pain), futile attempts at vomiting, and increased salivation. Bloat usually occurs when the dog is exercised too soon after eating. They will eat up to 4-6 cups of food at a time.

History

Airedale, a valley (dale) in the West Riding of Yorkshire, named for the river Aire that runs through it, was the birthplace of the breed. In the mid-19th Century, working class people created the Airedale Terrier by crossing the old English rough-coated Black and Tan Terrier (now known as the Welsh Terrier) with the Otterhound. In 1886, the Kennel Club of England formally recognized the Airedale Terrier breed.

In 1864 they were exhibited for the first time at a championship dog show sponsored by the Airedale Agricultural Society. They were classified under different names, including Rough Coated, Bingley and Waterside Terrier. In 1879 breed fanciers decided to call the breed the Airedale Terrier, a name accepted by the Kennel Club (England) in 1886.

Well-to-do hunters of the era were typically accompanied by a pack of hounds and several terriers, often running them both together. The hounds would scent and pursue the quarry and the terriers would "go to ground" or enter into the quarry's burrow and make the kill. Terriers were often the sporting dog of choice for the common man. Early sporting terriers needed to be big enough to tackle the quarry, but not so big as to prevent them from maneuvering through the quarry's underground lair. As a result, these terriers had to have a very high degree of courage and pluck to face the foe in a tight, dark underground den without the help of human handlers.

During the middle of the nineteenth century, regular sporting events took place along the Aire River in which terriers pursued the large river rats that inhabited the area. A terrier was judged on its ability to locate a "live" hole in the riverbank and then, after the rat was driven from its hole by a ferret brought along for that purpose, the terrier would pursue the rat through water until it could make a kill. As these events became more popular, demand arose for a terrier that could excel in this activity. One such terrier was developed through judicious crossings of the Black-and-Tan Terrier and Bull and Terrier dogs popular at the time with the Otter Hound. The result was a long-legged fellow that would soon develop into the dog we recognize today as the Airedale Terrier. This character was too big to "go to ground" in the manner of the smaller working terriers; however, it was good at everything else expected of a sporting terrier, and it was particularly adept at water work. This big terrier had other talents in addition to its skill as a ratter. Because of its hound heritage it was blessed with the ability to scent game and the size to be able to tackle larger animals. It became more of a multipurpose terrier that could pursue game by powerful scenting ability, be broken to gun, and taught to retrieve. Its size and temperament made it an able guardian of farm and home. One of the colorful, but less-than legal, uses of the early Airedale Terrier was to assist its master in poaching game on the large estates that were off-limits to commoners. Rabbits, hare, and fowl were plentiful, and the Airedale could be taught to retrieve game killed by its master, or to pursue, kill, and bring it back itself.

The first imports of Airedale Terriers to North America were in the 1880s. The first Airedale to come to American shores was named Bruce. After his 1881 arrival, Bruce won the terrier class in a New York dog show.

The patriarch of the breed is considered to be CH Master Briar (1897–1906). Two of his sons, Crompton Marvel and Monarch, also made important contributions to the breed.

The first Canadian registrations are recorded in the Stud book of 1888–1889.

In 1910, the ATCA (Airedale Terrier Club of America) offered the Airedale Bowl as a perpetual trophy, which continues to this day. It is now mounted on a hardwood pedestal base, holding engraved plates with the names of the hundreds of dogs that have been awarded Best of Breed at the National Specialties.

The Airedale was extensively used in World War I to carry messages to soldiers behind enemy lines and transport mail. They were also used by the Red Cross to find wounded soldiers on the battlefield. There are numerous tales of Airedales delivering their messages despite terrible injury. An Airedale named 'Jack' ran through half a mile of enemy fire, with a message attached within his collar. He arrived at headquarters with his jaw broken and one leg badly splintered, and right after he delivered the message, he dropped dead in front of its recipient.

Lieutenant Colonel Edwin Hautenville Richardson was responsible for the development of messenger and guard dogs in the British Army. He, along with his wife, established a War Dog Training School at Shoeburyness in Essex, England. In 1916, they provided two Airedales (Wolf & Prince)for use as message carriers. After both dogs proved themselves in battle, Airedales were given more duties, such as locating injured soldiers on the battlefield, an idea taken from the Red Cross.

Before the adoption of the German Shepherd as the dog of choice for law enforcement and search and rescue work, the Airedale terrier often filled this role.

In 1906, Richardson tried to interest the British Police in using dogs to accompany officers, for protection on patrol at night. Mr. Geddes, Chief Goods Manager for Hull Docks in Yorkshire, was convinced after he went saw the impressive work of police dogs in Belgium. Geddes convinced Superintendent Dobie of the North Eastern Railway Police, to arrange a plan for policing the docks. Airedale Terriers were selected for duty as police dogs because of their intelligence, good scenting abilities and their hard, wiry coats that were easy to maintain and clean.

At the beginning of the Russo-Japanese war in 1904, the Russian embassy in London contacted Lt. Colonel Richardson for help acquiring dogs for the Russian Army, trained to take the wounded away from the battlefields. He sent terriers, mostly Airedale Terriers, for communication and sanitary services. Although these original imports perished, Airedale Terriers were reintroduced to Russia in the early 1920s for use by the Red Army. Special service dog units were created in 1923, and Airedale Terriers were used as demolition dogs, guard dogs, police tracking dogs and casualty dogs.

Two Airedales were among the dogs lost with the sinking of the RMS Titanic. The Airedale "Kitty" belonged to Colonel John Jacob Astor IV, the real-estate mogul. The second Airedale belonged to William E. Carter of Bryn Mawr, Pennsylvania. Mr. Carter was the owner of the Renault automobile in which Jack and Rose trysted in the movie "Titanic". Carter, his wife and two children survived the sinking.

During the 1930s, when airedales were farmed like livestock, American breeders developed the Oorang airedale.

Capt. Walter Lingo, of LaRue, Ohio, developed the Oorang Airedale strain. The name came from a line of bench champions, headed by King Oorang 11, a dog which was said to have been the finest utility dog. King could retrieve waterfowl and upland game, tree raccoons, drive cattle and sheep, and bay mountain lions, bears, and wolves. King even fought one of the best fighting bull terriers, and killed his opponent. He also trained in Red Cross work, and served the American Expeditionary Force at the front in France.

Lingo simply wasn't satisfied with the average strain of Airedale, and after an incredible series of breedings, for which he brought in great Airedales from all over the world, he created the "King Oorang." At the time, Field and Stream magazine called it, "the greatest utility dog in the history of the world." The Oorang Kennel Company continued until Walter Lingo's death in 1969. To help promote the King Oorang, as well as his kennels, Lingo created the Oorang Indians football team headed up by Jim Thorpe. The team played in National Football League from 1922–1923. Jerry Siebert, an Airedale breeder in Buckeye Lake, Ohio, followed in Lingo's footsteps, and bred "Jerang Airedales." There is a kennel in Tennessee that claims to have original Oorang Airedales.

Dogs of close to 100 pounds and upwards may carry the medical and behavioral problems associated with the 1930s airedale. Many large airedales can be as robust, energetic and agile as much smaller dogs with the same life span as smaller airedales.

After the First World War, the Airedales' popularity rapidly increased thanks to stories of their bravery on the battlefield and also because Presidents Theodore Roosevelt, Calvin Coolidge, and Warren Harding owned Airedales. President Harding's Airedale was named Laddie Boy.

President Roosevelt claimed that "An Airedale can do anything any other dog can do and then lick the other dog, if he has to."

1949 marked the peak of the Airedales' popularity in the USA, ranked 20th out of 110 breeds by the American Kennel Club. The breed has since slipped to 50th out of 146.

Marion Robert Morrison, otherwise known as John Wayne, grew up in Glendale, California. His neighbors called him "Big Duke," because he never went anywhere without his Airedale Terrier, "Little Duke". He preferred "Duke" to "Marion," and the name stuck for the rest of his life.

The Airedale Terrier was recognized by United Kennel Club in 1914.

The Airedale Terrier, because of its joyful disposition and energy, was one of the first breeds, along with the Giant Schnauzer and the Rottweiler, used to create the Black Russian Terrier.

The Airedale is the current mascot for Alma High School (Alma, Arkansas).

One of the Giles Family, cornerstone characters of Carl Giles' cartoon series from the Daily Express in England, included Butch, an Airedale Terrier.

Further reading

- Tells the story of the Oorang Kennel operation in LaRue, Ohio, run by Walter Lingo.
- Cites the Airedale as a police dog and as a dispatch bearer in war.

American Staffordshire Terrier

The **American Staffordshire terrier** is a breed of medium-sized, short-coated dog whose early ancestors came from England. In the early part of the twentieth century, the breed gained respectability, and it was accepted by the American Kennel Club as Staffordshire Terrier.

History

Origins

Although the early ancestors of this breed came from England, the development of the American Staffordshire Terrier is the story of a truly American breed. This type of dog was instrumental in the success of farmers and settlers who developed this country. They were used for general farm work, guarding the homestead, and general companionship.

A number of the early ancestors were also developed for the "sport" of dog fighting. The extraordinary vitality of this breed is a direct result of breeding for successful fighting dogs.

Until the early part of the 19th century the Bulldog was bred with great care in England for the purpose of baiting bulls. Pictures from as late as 1870 represent the Bulldog of that day more like the present-day American Staffordshire Terrier than like the present-day Bulldog. Some writers contend it was the White English Terrier, or the Black and Tan Terrier, that was used as a cross with the Bulldog to perfect the Staffordshire Terrier. It seems easier to believe that any game terrier, such as the Fox Terrier of the early 1800s, was used in this cross, since some of the foremost authorities on dogs of that time state that the Black-and-Tan and the white English Terrier were none too game, but these same authorities go on to stress the gameness of the Fox Terrier. In analyzing the three above-mentioned terriers at that time, we find that there was not a great deal of difference in body conformation, the greatest differences being in color, aggressiveness, and spirit. In any event, it was the cross between the Bulldog and the terrier that resulted in the Staffordshire Terrier, which was originally called the Bull-and-Terrier Dog, Half and Half, and at times Pit Dog or Pit Bullterrier. Later, it assumed the name of Staffordshire Bull Terrier in England. These dogs began to find their way into America as early as 1870 where they became known as Pit Dog, Pit Bull Terrier, later American Bull Terrier, and still later as Yankee Terrier.

Popularity

American Staffordshire terriers reached a peak of popularity in the first half of the 20th century; "Pete the Pup" appeared in the Our Gang comedies, and the breed personified the all-American pet and soon spread all over the country.

In 1936, they were accepted for registration in the AKC Stud Book as Staffordshire Terriers. They belong to the terrier and molosser groups. The name of the breed was revised effective January 1, 1972 to American Staffordshire Terrier. Breeders in this country had developed a type which is heavier in weight than the Staffordshire Bull Terrier of England and the name change was to distinguish them as separate breeds.

Although ancestors of the American Staffordshire were fighting dogs, the selective breeding since the 1930s has been away from the fighting heritage. The American Staffordshire Terrier of today is a companion and show dog, rather than a gladiator. Although more rarely used on the farm now, the talents that made him a good all purpose dog are still to be found in the breed. Often called Amstaffs by breed enthusiasts, the dogs' popularity began to decline in the United States following World War II in favor of other breeds. Today the breed is ranked 66 among 155 dog breeds in the USA.

Temperament

The American Temperament Test Society conducts tests every year on thousands of dogs to determine the soundness of their temperament. The American Staffordshire Terrier routinely ranks well above many "popular" breeds such as the Beagle, Collie, Doberman Pinscher and the Cocker Spaniel. This is a very intelligent, human-oriented, active dog and an affectionate family pet. Over the past 50 years, careful breeding has produced this friendly, trustworthy dog. One of the characteristics that most owners and breeders talked and look for particular in this breed is gameness. Gameness refers to perseverance, spirited, readiness of a dog to accomplish a given task.

Health and well-being

Amstaff pups should not be brought home before they are 8–10 weeks old. Their life expectancy is generally 12 to 16 years with good care. It is a healthy breed with relatively few major problems. Notable issues related to health and wellbeing include:

Inherited disorders

* Amstaffs may suffer from Congenital Heart Disease (OFA rank:11, Percent Abnormal 1.6%, Percent Normal 95.1%)

* Amstaffs are somewhat prone to Canine hip dysplasia, though not as much as some other breeds. Hip scores are recommended before breeding. (OFA rank:21, Percent Abnormal 26.0%, Percent Normal 71.7%)

- Elbow dysplasia (OFA rank:12, Percent Abnormal 17.8%, Percent Normal 81.4%)
- There are some risk of knee problems. A luxating patella is a common occurrence in the knee where the leg is often bow shaped. (OFA rank:72, Percent Abnormal 1.3%, Percent Normal 98.7%)
- Thyroid Dysfunction (OFA rank:19, Percent Abnormal 8.0%, Percent Normal 80.0%)
- There is a small incidence of other conditions, such as senior ataxia and hereditary cataracts.

Other disorders

Amstaffs are sometimes prone to skin allergies, UTI, and Autoimmune diseases. Spondylosis and Osteoarthritis are common place in older dogs.

Breed-specific legislation

The American Staffordshire Terrier is often subject to breed bans worldwide that target the Bull and Terrier family in response to a number of well-publicized incidents involving pit bull-type dogs or other dog breeds. This legislation ranges from outright bans on the possession of these dogs to restrictions and conditions on ownership. However, the appropriateness and effectiveness of breed-specific legislation in preventing dog bite fatalities and injuries is disputed. Most animal-related organizations also oppose breed-specific legislation:

- **The American Veterinary Medical Association** supports dangerous animal legislation by state, county, or municipal governments provided that legislation **does not refer to specific breeds** or classes of animals.
- **Canadian Veterinary Medical Association** supports dangerous dog legislation provided that it does not refer to specific breeds.
- **The Centers for Disease Control** said that breed-specific approaches to the control of dog bites do not address the issue that many breeds are involved in the problem and that most of the factors contributing to dog bites are related to the level of responsibility exercised by dog owners. Furthermore, tethered dogs are more likely to bite than untethered dogs.
- **Journal of the American Veterinary Medical Association** states that because of difficulties inherent in determining a dog's breed with certainty, enforcement of breed-specific ordinances raises constitutional and practical issues.
- **SPCA** recognizes that dog bites are a serious public safety problem. Their interest in this issue relates directly to the goal of creating humane communities where people and animals enrich each other's lives. However, the BC SPCA opposes breed banning as a strategy for achieving this goal. Breed banning is a simplistic and ineffective solution to a multi-faceted problem.

Famous American Staffordshire Terriers

- Pete the Pup in several Our Gang films (later known as The Little Rascals) during the 1920s and 1930s.
- 'Jake', a dog, featured in an "easter egg"; hidden in DVD format for the horror film Cabin Fever.
- Sergeant Stubby died on March 16, 1926, as a hero. Sergeant Stubby is the most decorated dog in military history, and the only dog to have been promoted during battle. He fought for 18 months in the trenches for France during WW1 for 17 battles. Stubby warned his fellow soldiers of gas attacks, located wounded soldiers in No Man's Land, and listened for oncoming artillery rounds. He was also responsible for the capture of a German spy at Argonne. After his time in the war, Stubby met Woodrow Wilson, Calvin Coolidge, and Warren G. Harding. He was awarded life memberships to the American Legion, the Red Cross, and the YMCA.
- Jack Brutus was another famous military dog. He was the official mascot of Company K, First Connecticut Volunteer Infantry.
- "Bud" was the first dog to take a cross-country drive in 1903 with his owner Horatio Nelson Jackson and a bicycle mechanic named Sewall Crocker. "Bud soon became an enthusiast for motoring," Jackson bragged, especially after his masters put a pair of their goggles on him to keep the stinging, alkali dust out of his eyes.
- Poster image for the U.S. during the 1900s. This breed was the image people saw on various war posters, representing the country's strength and dignity.
- Is the only dog to have ever graced the cover of Life Magazine three times.

Books

- The American Staffordshire Terrier by Clifford & Alberta Ormsby, 1956
- American Staffordshire Terrier by Joseph Janish, 2003, 155 pages; ISBN 1593782489
- American Staffordshire Terrier Champions, 1988-1995 by Jan Linzy, 1998, 84 pages; ISBN 155893054X
- American Staffordshire Terrier Champions, 1996-2001 by Jan Linzy, 2002, 84 pages; ISBN 1558931023
- Staffordshire Terriers: American Staffordshire Terrier and Staffordshire Bull Terrier by Anna Katherine Nicholas, 1991, 256 pages; ISBN 0866226370
- The American Staffordshire Terrier: Gamester and Guardian by Sarah Foster, 1998, 139 pages; ISBN 0876050038

External links

- American Kennel Club - American Staffordshire Terrier information [1]
- American Staffordshire Terrier Forum [2]
- Staffordshire Terrier Club of America [3]

Australian Terrier

The **Australian Terrier** is a small sized breed of dog of the terrier dog type. The breed was developed in Australia, although the ancestral types of dogs from which the breed descends were from Great Britain.

Appearance

The Australian Terrier is a small dog with short legs, weighing around approx. 6.5 kg (14 lbs) and standing about 25 cms (10 ins.) at the withers, with a medium length shaggy harsh double coat that is not normally trimmed. Fur is shorter on the muzzle, lower legs, and feet, and there is a ruff around the neck. The coat colours are shades of blue or red with a lighter coloured topknot, and with markings on face, ears, body and legs of a colour described in the breed standard as "tan, never sandy". The tail was traditionally docked. As with most pet dog breeds, all proportions and aspects of the body and head as well as colours and markings are extensively described in the breed standard.

History

The Australian Terrier is descended from the rough coated type terriers brought from Great Britain to Australia in the early 1800s. The ancestral types of all of these breeds were kept to eradicate mice and rats. The Australian Terrier shares ancestors with the Cairn Terrier, Shorthaired Skye Terrier, and the Dandie Dinmont Terrier; Yorkshire Terriers and Irish Terriers were also crossed into the dog during the breed's development.

Development of the breed began in Tasmania about 1820, and the dogs were at first called the Rough Coated Terrier. The breed was officially recognised with the founding of the first breed club in 1887, and the breed was recognised as the Australian Terrier in 1892. The Australian Terrier was shown at a dog show for the first time in 1903 in Melbourne, and was also shown in Great Britain about the same time. The Kennel Club (UK) recognised the breed in 1933. The American Kennel Club recognised the Australian Terrier in 1960, and the United Kennel Club (US) in 1969. It is now recognised by all of the major kennel clubs in the English speaking world, and also is listed by various minor kennel clubs and other clubs and registries.

Health

There are three completed health surveys for Australian Terriers. Two surveys, one in 1997 and one in 2002, have been conducted by the Australian Terrier Club of America. The Club is currently collecting data for their next survey. The UK Kennel Club has a 2004 survey, but it has a much smaller sample size than the Australian Terrier Club of America surveys. Some of the respondents in the American surveys were from Australia, but there is no separate Australian health survey.

Mortality

In both 1997 and 2002 Australian Terrier Club of America surveys, median longevity of Australian Terriers was 11 years (total sample size of 230 deceased dogs). In the Kennel Club (UK) 2004 survey, median longevity was 12.1 years, but the sample size was only 11 deceased dogs. 11 years is a typical median longevity for purebred dogs in general, but on the low end of longevities for breeds similar in size to Australian Terriers.

Major causes of death in the 2002 survey were cancer (67%), old age (17%), undetermined (16%), and diabetes (13%).

Morbidity

Among 619 living dogs in the 2002 Australian Terrier Club of America survey, the most commonly reported health problems were endocrine (primarily diabetes), allergic dermatitis, and musculoskeletal (primarily luxating patella and ruptured cranial cruciate ligament). Other conditions reported among more than 4% of the surveyed dogs were adult onset cataracts and ear infections. The much smaller 2004 UKC survey, with 28 living dogs, suggested similar health concerns.

Temperament

The breed standard describes the ideal Australian Terrier temperament as spirited, alert, "with the natural aggressiveness of a ratter and hedge hunter". Aussies rank 34th in Stanley Coren's *The Intelligence of Dogs*, being of above average "Working and Obedience" intelligence, indicating good trainability. As with other terriers, they can be dog-aggressive and somewhat bossy, and care must be taken when living in a multi-pet household. In general, adult male terriers do not get along well with other adult male dogs. Since the Australian Terrier was also bred for companionship, they tend to be very people friendly, and enjoy interacting with people.

See also

- Terrier
- Terrier Group

Bedlington Terrier

The **Bedlington Terrier** is a breed of terrier named after the mining town of Bedlington, Northumberland in North East England.

Description

Appearance: The Bedlington Terrier is often described as looking like a lamb on a leash, probably because it has non-shedding fur with a woolly texture. These dogs may be blue, sandy, liver, or dark brown/black and sable and can be solid colours or have tan markings.

This breed has a wedge-shaped head with sparkling, triangular eyes.Its body shape, however, is unusual for a terrier, being somewhat like a Greyhound in construction, which enables it to gallop at great speed. However, the front legs are constructed differently from those quick hounds in that, the front legs are closer together at the feet than at the elbows - creating a triangular shape when viewed from the front. This enables them to turn or pivot quickly when chasing quarry at high speed. They are groomed with long hair left on the top of their skull and muzzle, tassels on the ears and slightly longer furnishings on the legs than the body coat.The quarry, trying to escape, would bite at the dog, and the hair saved the Bedlington from an injury to the important facial area and possible death from an infection. A similar idea is seen in the tail, crest and wings of the Secretary Bird.

Temperament

Calmer and less boisterous than many other terriers, the Bedlington Terrier is known as a dog with a good nature and mild manners. In addition, it is fast enough to bay a badger or a fox and is a first-rate water dog. Incredibly smart and attentive to its owner, the Bedlington is one of the most reliable terriers. They are problem solvers and loyal family companions.

Like most dogs, if left alone with nothing to do they can become destructive and need exercise; however, they make good dogs for small homes like apartments as long as they get walks and attention. They can make cheerful, lovely companions, and are eager to please.

Care

Grooming

Weekly combing and professional grooming are needed every 6-8 weeks to keep their coats (which tend to curl) in good shape. Dogs being prepared for the show ring often have much more hair left on them than those in "pet clips," which provide pet owners with a more manageable trim for their pets. The show trim is entirely hand-scissored, with the exception of the ears, face/throat, belly and tail which are trimmed with an electric clipper. It can take years to master the grooming pattern for this breed.

Exercise

These high-energy dogs need walks and aerobic play sessions daily to keep them happy and content. The breed is well suited for agility, earthdog, obedience and other performance events.

Hypoallergenic qualities

Bedlington Terriers often appear on lists of dogs that do not shed (moult), but this is misleading. Every hair in the dog coat grows from a hair follicle, which has a cycle of growing, then dying and being replaced by another follicle. When the follicle dies, the hair is shed. The length of time of the growing and shedding cycle varies by breed, age, and by whether the dog is an inside or outside dog. "There is no such thing as a nonshedding breed." The grooming of the Bedlington helps remove loose hair, and the curl in the coat helps prevent dead hair and dander from escaping into the environment, as with the poodle's coat. The frequent brushing and bathing required to keep the Bedlington looking its best removes hair and dander and controls the other potent allergen, saliva. Although hair, dander, and saliva can be minimized, they are still present and can stick to "clothes and the carpets and furnishings in your home"; inhaling them, or being licked by the dog, can trigger a reaction in a sensitive person.

History

The famed progenitor of Bedlington was a dog named "Old Flint", whelped in 1782 and owned by "Squire Trevelyan." Originally, the breed was known as the "Rothbury" or "Rodbery Terrier." This name derived from a famous bitch brought from Staffordshire by a company of nail makers who settled in Rothbury. The Terriers of this section were accustomed to rodent hunting underground, and worked with packs of foxhounds kept there at the time.

It is suggested that the Bedlington may well have made its way to Ireland and played a part in the early development of the Kerry Blue Terrier.

The first Bedlington Terrier club was formed in 1877. The Bedlington Terrier was recognized by the United Kennel Club in 1948.

Ch. Femars' Cable Car, descendant of Ch. Rock Ridge Night Rocket winner of best-in-show at the Westminster Kennel Club Dog Show in 1948, was featured on the cover of Sports Illustrated in the February 8, 1960 edition.

Health

Mortality

Median longevity of Bedlington Terriers, based on two recent UK surveys, is about 13.5 years, which is longer than for purebred dogs in general and longer than most breeds similar in size. The longest-lived of 48 deceased dogs in a 2004 UK Kennel Club survey was 18.4 years. Leading causes of death among Bedlington Terriers in the UK were old age (23%), urologic (15%), and hepatic (12.5%). The leading "hepatic" cause of death was copper toxicosis. Dogs that died of liver diseases usually died at a younger age than dogs dying of most other causes.

Morbidity

Bedlington Terrier owners in the UK reported that the most common health issues among living dogs were reproductive (primarily of concern to breeders), heart murmur, and eye problems such as epiphora and cataracts. Copper toxicosis occurred among about 5% of living dogs.

Copper Toxicosis; Copper Storage Disease

Bedlington Terriers have an unusually high incidence of copper toxicosis, an inherited autosomal recessive disease, characterized by accumulation of excess copper in the liver. Genetic testing is now available, and the disease has been largely bred out of the Bedlington population in the United States. Active disease (rather than inheritance) is diagnosed with a liver biopsy. It is essential that anyone interested in purchasing a Bedlington is provided with proof of the dogs' unaffected status.

External links

- Bedlington Terrier Club of America, Inc. [1]
- National Bedlington Terrier Club (UK) [2]
- Bedlington Terrier Association (UK) [3]
- Bedlington Terrier health Group (UK) [4]

Border Terrier

A **Border Terrier** is a small, rough-coated breed of dog of the terrier group. Originally bred as fox and vermin hunters, Border Terriers share ancestry with Dandie Dinmont Terriers and Bedlington Terriers.

Though the breed is much older, the Border Terrier was officially recognized by the The Kennel Club in Great Britain in 1920, and by the American Kennel Club (AKC) in 1930.

In 2006, the Border Terrier ranked 81st in number of registrations by the AKC, while it ranked 10th in the United Kingdom.

In 2008, the Border Terrier ranked 8th in number of registrations by the UK Kennel Club.

Description

Appearance

Identifiable by their otter-shaped heads, Border Terriers have a broad skull and short, strong muzzle with a scissors bite. The V-shaped ears are on the sides of the head and fall towards the cheeks. Common coat colors are grizzle-and-tan, blue-and-tan, red, or wheaten. Whiskers are few and short. The tail is naturally moderately short, thick at the base and tapering.

Narrow-bodied and well-proportioned, males stand at the shoulder, and weigh ; females and .

The Border Terrier has a double coat consisting of a short, dense, soft undercoat and harsh, wiry weather and dirt resistant, close-lying outer coat with no curl or wave. This coat usually requires hand-stripping twice a year to remove dead hair. It then takes about eight weeks for the top coat to come back in. For some dogs, weekly brushing will suffice. Most Border Terriers are seen groomed with short hair but longer hair can sometimes be preferred.

Temperament

Though sometimes stubborn and strong willed; border terriers are, on the whole very even tempered, and are rarely aggressive. Border Terriers generally get along well with other dogs and are often good with children.

Borders do well in task-oriented activities and have a surprising ability to jump high and run fast given the size of their legs. The breed has excelled in agility training, but they are quicker to learn jumps and see-saws than weaving poles. They take training for tasks very well, but appear less tractable if being taught mere tricks.

They are intelligent and eager to please, but they retain the capacity for independent thinking and initiative that were bred into them for working rats and fox underground. Their love of people and even temperament make them fine therapy dogs, especially for children and the elderly, and they are occasionally used to aid the blind or deaf. From a young age they should be trained on command.

Borders can adapt to different environments and situations well, and are able to deal with temporary change well. They will get along well with cats that they have been raised with, but may chase other cats and small animals such as mice, rabbits, squirrels, rats, and guinea pigs.

Borders love to sit and watch what is going on. Walks with Borders will often involve them sitting and lying in the grass to observe the environment around them. They can be stubborn when they are tired and often require short breaks to sit and observe during long walks; it can be difficult to get them moving again.

Health

Borders are a generally hardy breed, though there are certain genetic health problems associated with them, including:

- Hip dysplasia
- Perthes disease
- Various heart defects
- Juvenile cataracts
- Progressive retinal atrophy
- Seizures
- Canine Epileptoid Cramping Syndrome (CECS)

Border Terriers are also known to be sensitive to anaesthetics and slow to induce.

Due to their instinct to kill and consume smaller animals, Border Terriers often destroy, and sometimes eat, toys that are insufficiently robust. Indigestion resulting from eating a toy can cause the appearance of illness. Typical symptoms include lethargy, unwillingness to play, a generally 'unhappy' appearance, lack of reaction to affection, and inability or unwillingness to sleep. These symptoms are generally very noticeable, however, they are also present just prior to Border Terrier bitches being on heat. They are strong-willed, very lively, and also like running.

Earthdog trials

Border Terriers have earned more American Kennel Club (AKC) Earthdog titles than any other terrier. An AKC earthdog test is not true hunting, but an artificial, non-competitive, exercise in which terriers enter wide smooth wooden tunnels, buried under-ground, with one or more turns in order to bark or scratch at caged rats that are safely housed behind wooden bars. The tests are conducted to determine that instinctive traits are preserved and developed, as the breed originators intended for the dogs to their work. While earthdog tests are not a close approximation of hunting, they are popular in the U.S. and in some European countries because even over-large Kennel Club breeds can negotiate the tunnels with ease, dogs can come to no harm while working, and no digging is required. Since Border Terriers are "essentially working terriers", many Border Terrier owners consider it important to test and develop their dogs' instinct. These tests also provide great satisfaction for the dogs. The American Working Terrier Association (AWTA) does conduct "trials"; where the dogs instincts are tested, and then judged to determine a "Best of Breed" Earthdog. These trials are also run similar as described below.

History

The Border Terrier originates in, and takes its name from the Scottish borders. Their original purpose was to bolt foxes which had gone to ground. They were also used to kill rodents, but they have been used to hunt otters and badgers too.

The first Kennel Club Border Terrier ever registered was The Moss Trooper, a dog sired by Jacob Robson's Chip in 1912 and registered in the Kennel Club's Any Other Variety listing in 1913. The Border Terrier was rejected for formal Kennel Club recognition in 1914, but won its slot in 1920, with the first standard being written by Jacob Robson and John Dodd. Jasper Dodd was made first President of the Club.

Famous Border Terriers

- Puffy in *There's Something About Mary*
- Puffy's female offspring Raleigh, Clay Aiken's pet dog
- Baxter in *Anchorman: The Legend of Ron Burgundy*
- Hubble in *Good Boy!*
- Co-star in *Lassie* (Named "Toots")
- Seymour in *Futurama* as main character Philip J. Fry's pet dog when he worked at Pinucchi's Pizza
- Lady Eccles in *Coronation Street* as Blanch's inheritance gift from her friend
- Scamp in *The Suite Life of Zack & Cody* as Maddie's scruffy dog who falls in love with London Tipton's *Pomeranian*, Ivana
- Shep Proudfoot, Greg Laswell's pet dog
- Mackenzie, the dog of the Champion
- Nancy in *Unfabulous* as Addie's pet dog
- Chomp in *102 Dalmatians*
- Tansy as Toto from Return To Oz (1985 Disney film)

References

Eccles in Coronation Street (uk)

External links

- Canine Epileptoid Cramping Syndrome [1]
- Border Terrier Club of America - BTCA [2]
- Border Terrier Canada [3]
- Border Terrier Show Results in the U.K. [4]

Bull Terrier

The **Bull Terrier** or **English Bull Terrier** is a breed of dog in the terrier family. They are known for their large, egg-shaped head, small triangular eyes and their "jaunty gait." Their temperament has been described as generally fun-loving, active and clownish. Bull terriers have appeared as characters in many cartoons, books, movies, and advertisements, perhaps most famously as party loving Spuds MacKenzie in Budweiser beer commercials in the late 1980s, and more recently as the Target dog.

Description

Appearance

The Bull Terrier's most recognizable feature is its head, described as 'egg shaped' when viewed from the front, almost flat at the top, with a Roman muzzle sloping evenly down to the end of the nose with no stop. The unique triangle-shaped eyes are small, dark, and deep-set. The body is full and round, while the shoulders are robust and muscular and the tail is carried horizontally. It walks with a jaunty gait, and is popularly known as the 'gladiator of the canine race'.

There is no designated height or weight for the breed, but the average is, Height: 51–61 cm (20-24 inches), Weight: 20–38 kg (44-85 pounds) The Bull Terrier and the Miniature Bull Terrier are the only recognized breeds that have triangle-shaped eyes.

Temperament

Though this breed was once known as fierce gladiator, it is much gentler today. A Bull Terrier might have a preventive effect and it will certainly defend its owner in a truly critical situation. Bull terriers are known to be courageous, scrappy, fun-loving, active, clownish and fearless. The Bull Terrier tends to be a loyal and polite dog. They become very attached to their owners. The Bull Terrier thrives on firm, consistent leadership and affection. They generally like to stay occupied, and fit in well with active families where they receive a great deal of companionship and supervision. They tend not do well in situations where they are left alone for 8 hours a day. This breed can be a wonderful pet if very thoroughly socialized and trained, but not recommended for most households. They are fond of people of all ages, but if they do not get enough physical and mental exercise they may be too energetic for small children. Children should be taught how to display leadership towards the dog. Meek owners will find them to become very protective, willful, possessive and/or jealous. Bull Terriers may try to join into family rough housing or quarrel. Bull Terriers generally must be given a lot of structure. Unless the owner can ensure socialization and constantly maintain a pack leader mentality, they can be extremely aggressive with other dogs. Unaltered males may not get along with other male dogs. Males and females can live together happily, and two females can also be a good combination with care and supervision. They are not recommended with other non-canine pets such as cats, hamsters, and guinea pigs. They can make excellent watch dogs.

Health

All puppies should be checked for deafness, which occurs in 20% of pure white dogs and 1.3% of colored dogs and is difficult to notice, especially in a relatively young puppy. Many Bull Terriers have a tendency to develop skin allergies. Insect bites, such as those from fleas, and sometimes mosquitoes and mites, can produce a generalized allergic response of hives, rash, and itching. This problem can be stopped by keeping the dog free of contact from these insects, but this is definitely a consideration in climates or circumstances where exposure to these insects is inevitable. Their average lifespan is around 10–12 years, although they may live longer - a male bull terrier house pet in South Wales, UK by the name of "Buller" lived to the age of 18 years. The oldest female Bull Terrier on record is an Australian house pet dubbed "Puppa Trout" who remained sprightly into her 17th year. The second oldest female Bull Terrier on record is "Boots Moon Stomp Stout (Crain)" of Denver, Colorado USA. Boots lived to be 16 years of age.

The Bull Terrier's coat is easy to maintain, but grooming can keep it in near-perfect condition. Adding oils to their meals can also vastly improve the quality of their coat. English Bull Terriers have thin, fine hair that requires minimal grooming. They are known to have light shedding patterns. Another important issue is that any whiteness around the eyes, ears, nose, mouth, stomach or hindquarters with a short and sparse haired breed such as this must be protected against the sun with a gentle but high SPF factored sunscreen to prevent sunburn and subsequent cancer. The Bull Terrier requires a fair amount of exercise, but overworking the dog at a young age will cause strained muscles. Older dogs do require exercise, but in small doses, whereas younger ones will be happy to play for hours on end. The breed is renowned for being extremely greedy.

Other common ailments: Umbilical Hernia and Acne. Bull Terriers can also suffer from obsessive compulsive disorder, such as tail chasing, self mutilation, and obsessive licking.

History

Early in the mid-1800s the "Bull and Terrier" breeds were developed to satisfy the needs for vermin control and animal-based blood sports. The "Bull and Terriers" were based on the Old English Bulldog (now extinct) and one or more of Old English Terrier and "Black and tan terrier", now known as Manchester Terrier. This new breed combined the speed and dexterity of lightly built terriers with the dour tenacity of the Bulldog, which was a poor performer in most combat situations, having been bred almost exclusively for killing bulls and bears tied to a post. Due to the lack of breed standards—breeding was for performance, not appearance—the "Bull and Terrier" eventually divided into the ancestors of "Bull Terriers" and "Staffordshire Bull Terriers", both smaller and easier to handle than the progenitor.

About 1850, James Hinks started breeding "Bull and Terriers" with "English White Terriers" (now extinct), looking for a cleaner appearance with better legs and nicer head. In 1862, Hinks entered a bitch called "Puss" sired by his white Bulldog called "Madman" into the Bull Terrier Class at the dog show held at the Cremorne Gardens in Chelsea. Originally known as the "Hinks Breed" and "The White Cavalier", these dogs did not yet have the now-familiar "egg face", but kept the stop in the skull profile.

The dog was immediately popular and breeding continued, using Dalmatian, Greyhound, Spanish Pointer, Foxhound and Whippet to increase elegance and agility; and Borzoi and Collie to reduce the stop. Hinks wanted his dogs white, and bred specifically for this. Generally, however, breeding was aimed at increasing sturdiness: three "subtypes" were recognised by judges, Bulldog, Terrier and Dalmatian, each with its specific conformation, and a balance is now sought between the three. The first modern Bull Terrier is now recognised as "Lord Gladiator", from 1917, being the first dog with no stop at all.

Due to medical problems associated with all-white breeding, Ted Lyon among others began introducing colour, using Staffordshire Bull Terriers in the early 20th century. Coloured Bull Terriers were recognised as a separate variety (at least by the AKC) in 1936. Brindle is the preferred colour, but other colours are welcome.

Along with conformation, specific behaviour traits were sought. The epithet "White Cavalier", harking back to an age of chivalry, was bestowed on a breed which while never seeking to start a fight was well able to finish one, while socialising well with its "pack", including children and pups. Hinks himself had always aimed at a "gentleman's companion" dog rather than a pit-fighter—though Bullies were often entered in the pits, with some success. Today the Bullie is valued as a comical, mischievous, imaginative and intelligent (problem-solving) but stubborn house pet suitable for experienced owners.

Bull Terrier facts

- The Afrikaans name for the Bull Terrier is *Varkhond*
- There is also a miniature version of this breed; this distinct breed is officially known as the Miniature Bull Terrier.
- Bull Terriers are prominently featured in Jonathan Carroll's 1980 novel *The Land of Laughs*.
- Bull Terriers have appeared in many movies, including: *A Dog's Life* (1918), It's a Dog's Life (1955), *Oliver!*, *Baxter*, *Patton*, *Toy Story*, *Babe: Pig in the City*, *Next Friday*, *Friday After Next*, *Frankenweenie*, *Trainspotting*, *Bulletproof*, *Derailed*, "Scotland, PA", *The Incredible Journey*, *Space Buddies* and *Snatch*.
- A Bull Terrier appears in several scenes of the 1976 film *Je t'aime... moi non plus*.
- Bull Terriers have also featured in television shows such as the 1970s television show *Baa Baa Black Sheep*, in the opening credits of the British television show *Barking Mad*, and in the short lived Fox series *Keen Eddie*.
- A Bull Terrier is the main character in a Max Brand novel "The White Wolf".
- Spuds Mackenzie, a dog featured in an advertising campaign for Bud Light beer in the late 1980s, was a bull terrier.
- American children's writer and illustrator Chris Van Allsburg features a bull terrier named Fritz in at least one scene in every book.

Famous Bull Terriers

- Abraxas Aaran, who portrayed Willie, the title character's dog, in the 1970 film *Patton*.
- Baxter, from the film *Baxter* - with the tagline, "Méfiez-vous du chien qui pense." ("Beware the dog that thinks.")
- Blue, owned by Canadian hockey commentator Don Cherry, is widely considered to be almost as famous as Cherry himself.
- Bodger, an old white bull terrier, is a major character in the book The Incredible Journey by Sheila Burnford and the movie
- Brut, in the novel, Answers to Brut, by Gillian Rubinstein
- In Charles Dickens' novel Oliver Twist, Bill Sykes owns an English Bull Terrier named Bullseye.
- Bullseye mascot of the Target Corporation
- Chester, Chad's (Preppy) dog in Rockstar Vancouver's video game Bully
- Chico, a dog in *Next Friday* and *Friday After Next*
- Creampuff, one of Irish Murphy's pig hunting dogs from the *Footrot Flats* comic series.
- Kirk Hammett of the thrash metal band Metallica has a bull terrier named Darla.
- Dave, an old white bull terrier of the Priory Estate.
- Hip-Hop artist Adil Omar has a bull terrier named Diablo.

- Fritz, the black-and-white bull terrier who appears in every Chris Van Allsburg book.
- Grimm, of the cartoon series Mother Goose and Grimm.
- Odd's dog, Kiwi, is rumored to be a bull terrier but he looks more like a Whippet.
- Jock, one of the most famous dogs in South Africa. He was the companion of the Percy Fitzpatrick. A book was written about him by Fitzpatrick, It was called Jock of the Bushveld.
- Lockjaw, Pepper's companion in Sierra's Pepper's Adventures in Time.
- Meatball, White bull terrier pet of Major Gregory "Pappy" Boyington in Baa Baa Black Sheep (TV series).
- Pete, from the Fox-television series "Keen Eddie", 13 episodes, 2003
- Rex from the film Stealing Harvard. Rex is a mean dog who always agrees with his master. However, his crankyness goes away when he tries to bite a man in the crotch and ends up falling in love and having sex with him.
- Rick Springfield's bull terrier Ronnie appears on the cover of his album *Working Class Dog*.
- Rude Dog
- Sam, who accompanied Alby Mangels, Dutch-Australian adventurer, on his world travels.
- Scud, from the Disney/Pixar film *Toy Story*.
- Sparky, the dog who appears in "Frankenweenie"
- Spuds MacKenzie - "star" of Bud Light beer commercials in the late 1980s
- Spunky, of *Rocko's Modern Life*, resembles a Bull Terrier and was also the name of a famous MA Bull Terrier.
- Sputnik from *Space Buddies*.
- Whiskey, from the Eidos Commandos series
- Willie, owned by World War II US Army General George S. Patton and named after William the Conqueror.
- Unnamed bull terriers regularly appearing in New Yorker cartoonist George Booth's cartoons.
- The dog from Angry Kid
- Mumps, the bull terrier who wanders around with Bob Jakin, a prominent character in the novel "The Mill on the Floss" by George Eliot.

See also

- Miniature Bull Terrier

External links

- Bullterrierssa.co.za [1], A complete encyclopedia
- Colouredbullterrierclub.com [2], UK Coloured Bull Terrier Club
- BullieSOS.co.uk [3]
- Bulldoginformation.com [4], Bull Terrier Info Page
- BulliesInNeed.org.uk [5], Rescuing and rehoming Bull Terriers in the UK since 2002
- BullTerrierRescue.org [6]
- DogsInDepth.com [7]

Cairn Terrier

The **Cairn Terrier** is one of the oldest terrier breeds, originating in the Scottish Highlands and recognized as one of Scotland's earliest working dogs. It is used for hunting and burrowing prey among the cairns.

Although the breed had existed long before, the name Cairn Terrier was a compromise suggestion after the breed was originally brought to official shows in the United Kingdom in 1909 under the name Short-haired Skye terriers. This name was not acceptable to The Kennel Club due to opposition from Skye Terrier breeders, and the name Cairn Terrier was suggested as an alternative. The Cairn Terrier quickly became popular and has remained so ever since. They are usually left-pawed. Cairn Terriers are ratters. In Ireland they would search the cairns (large rock piles) for rats and other rodents. Thus if one is kept as a house hold pet it will do the job of a cat, specifically catching and killing mice, rabbits, and squirrels.

Description

Appearance

Cairn Terrier physique	
Weight:	13-17 pounds (6–8 kg)
Height:	10–13 inches (25–33 cm)
Coat:	Abundant shaggy outer coat, soft downy undercoat
Litter size:	2-10
Life span:	12–15 years

The breed standard can be found Cairn Terrier Club of America website. The current standard was approved on May 10, 1938 and was adopted from The Kennel Club (UK). According to the American standard, dogs should weigh 14 pounds and stand 10" at the withers. Females should weigh 13 pounds and stand 9.5" at the withers. A Cairn's appearance may vary from this standard. It is common for a Cairn to stand between 9 and 13 inches (23–33 cm) at the withers and weigh 13 to 17 pounds (6 to 8 kg). European Cairns tend to be larger than American Cairns. Due to irresponsible breeding, many Cairns available today are much smaller or much larger than the breed standard. Cairns that have had puppy mill backgrounds can weigh as little as 7 pounds or as much as 27 pounds.

The Cairn Terrier has a harsh, weather-resistant outer coat that can be cream, wheaten, red, sandy, gray, or brindled in any of these colors. Pure black, black and tan, and white are not permitted by many kennel clubs. While registration of white Cairns was once permitted, after 1917 the American Kennel Club required them to be registered as West Highland White Terriers. A notable characteristic of Cairns is that brindled Cairns frequently change color throughout their lifetime. It is not uncommon for a brindled Cairn to become progressively more black or silver as it ages. The Cairn is double-coated, with a soft, dense undercoat and a harsh outer coat. A well-groomed Cairn has a rough-and-ready appearance, free of artifice or exaggeration. Also it has the appearance of its cousin the West Highland White Terreir

Temperament

Cairn Terriers are adventurous, intelligent, strong, and loyal. Like most terriers, they love to dig after real or imagined prey. Cairn Terriers have a strong prey instinct and will need comprehensive training. However, they are intelligent and, although willful, can be trained. Training of the Cairn Terrier has the best results when training as a puppy, as they become unwillfully stubborn. Although it is often said that they are disobedient, this is not the case provided correct training is applied.

Cairns are working dogs and are still used as such in parts of Scotland. Cairn Terriers generally adapt well to children and are suitable family dogs.

Cairne terriers are also found to be nervous and frightened when brought to a new home but with correct training he/she will finally break out of it.

Grooming

Cairn Terriers should always be hand stripped. Using scissors or shears can ruin the dog's rugged outer coat after one grooming. Hand stripping involves pulling the old dead hair out by the roots. This does not harm the dog in any way. Removing the dead hair in this manner allows new growth to come in. This new growth helps protect the dog from water and dirt. Extra attention should be given to the grooming of the Cairn Terrier in order to help prevent bothersome skin conditions as they get older. Be sure to see that the dog's skin is all right before grooming. Keeping any dog routinely groomed leads to better health.

Health

These dogs are generally healthy and live on average about fifteen years. Yet breeders, owners and veterinarians have identified several health problems that are significant for Cairns. Some of these diseases are hereditary while others occur as a result of nonspecific factors (i.e. infections, toxins, injuries, or advanced age).

Some of the more common hereditary health problems found in the Cairn are:

- Cataracts
- Ocular Melanosis
- Progressive retinal atrophy
- Corneal dystrophy
- Krabbe disease (Globoid cell leukodystrophy)
- Hip dysplasia
- Legg-Calvé-Perthes syndrome
- Craniomandibular osteopathy (Lion Jaw)
- Von Willebrand disease
- Hypothyroidism
- Portosystemic shunt
- Luxating patella
- Entropion
- Soft Tissue Sarcoma (STS)

Currently, the Cairn Terrier Club of America [1] along with the Institute for Genetic Disease Control in Animals [2] maintain an open registry for Cairn Terriers in hopes of reducing the occurrence of hereditary diseases within the breed. Breeders voluntarily submit their dogs' test results for research purpose, as well as for use by individuals who seek to make sound breeding decisions.

Mixes

- Bushland Terrier Scottie Cairn Mix

Famous Cairns

Terry, the dog who played Toto in the 1939 screen adaptation of *The Wizard of Oz*, was a Cairn Terrier. Due to the identification of the State of Kansas with the original story *The Wonderful Wizard of Oz*, a resident of Wichita, Kansas has begun a drive to make the Cairn Terrier the official dog of the State of Kansas. Cairn terriers have also appeared in other movies:

- *Bright Eyes*, 1934 (Terry)
- *The Wizard of Oz*, 1939 (Toto)
- *Calling Philo Vance* [3], 1940 (Terry)
- *Reap the Wild Wind*, 1942
- *George Washington Slept Here*, 1942 (Terry)
- *The Uninvited*, 1944
- *Without Love*, 1945
- *The Valley of Decision*, 1945
- *The Ghost and Mrs. Muir*, 1947
- *Saturn 3*, 1980
- *The Stepfather*, 1987
- *Graveyard Shift*, 1990
- *Hocus Pocus*, 1993
- *2 Days in the Valley*, 1996
- *Twister*, 1996
- *Dunston Checks In'*, 1996]
- *The Portrait of a Lady*, 1996
- *My Summer Vacation* [4], 1996
- *Lost & Found*, 1999
- *Children of Men*, 2006 (Appears at about 1 hour 6 minutes)

In media

- *I Love Lucy* - Little Ricky had a Cairn Terrier named Fred
- UK TV Presenter Paul O'Grady often features a Cairn Terrier called Olga on his prime time chat show; dark in colour, Olga was a rescue dog.
- Also in the UK, Pauline Fowler actress Wendy Richards in the BBC TV show *EastEnders* had a Cairn she fondly named "Betty".
- Australian television soap series *Neighbours* had a Cairn Terrier named Audrey who belonged to the character Libby Kennedy
- National Treasure 2
- Jiminy - Prized showdog in Ontario, Canada

In books

- In the *Maximum Ride* book series Total the talking dog is a Cairn Terrier.

References

Books

- Beynon, J. W. H. & Fisher, A. (1969). The Cairn Terrier 4th ed. revised. London: Popular Dogs. ISBN 0090614526.
- Beynon, J. W. H. & Fisher, A. (revised by Wilson, P.). (1977). The Cairn Terrier 6th ed. London: Popular Dogs Pub. Co. ISBN 0091293405.
- Beynon, J. W. H. & Hutchison, J. H. (1930). The Popular Cairn Terrier. London: Popular Dogs Pub. Co., Ltd. Accession No: OCLC: 10576671.
- Beynon, J. W. H., Fisher, A., Wilson, P. & Proudlock, D. (1988). The Terrier. Place of Publication Unknown: Popular Dogs. ISBN 0091581508.
- Birch, B. & Birch, R. (1999). Pet Owner's Guide to the Cairn Terrier. Sydney: Ringpress. ISBN 1860541119.
- Camino E.E. & B. Co. Cairn Terrier Champions, 1952-1986. Camino, CA: Camino E.E. & B. Co. ISBN 0940808471.
- Carter, C. (1995). The Cairn Terrier. Neptune, NJ: T.F.H. Accession No: OCLC: 34877430.
- Caspersz, T. W. L. (1957). The Cairn Terrier Handbook: Giving the Origin and History of the Breed, Its Show Career, Its Points and Breeding. London: Nicholson & Watson. Accession No: OCLC: 6756006.
- Cooke, R. & Cooke, C. (1997). The Cairn Terrier in Canada. East St. Paul, MB: R. & C. Cooke. : ISBN 096831760X (v. 1).
- Gordon, J. F. (1988). All About the Cairn Terrier. London: Pelham Books ISBN 0720717868.
- Jacobi, G. A. (1976). Your Cairn Terrier. Fairfax, VA: Denlinger's. ISBN 0877140391.

- Jamieson, R. (2000). Cairn Terrier. Dorking: Interpet. ISBN 1902389344.
- Lehman, P. F. (1999). Cairn Terriers. Hauppauge, NY : Barron's Educational Series. ISBN 0764106384.
- Marcum, B. E. (1995). The New Cairn Terrier. New York : Howell Book House. ISBN 0876050739.
- Marvin, J. T. (1986). The New Complete Cairn Terrier 2nd ed. New York: Howell Book House. ISBN 0876050976.
- McCormack, E. (1983). How to Raise and Train a Cairn Terrier. Neptune, N.J.: T.F.H. Publications. ISBN 0876662629.
- Patten, B. J. (1996). The Terrier Breeds. Vero Beach, FL: Rourke Corp. ISBN 0865934584.
- Ross, F. M., Burton, N. L. & others. (1932). The Cairn Terrier. Manchester, England: "Our Dogs" Pub. Co. Accession No: OCLC: 19603882.
- Schneider, E. (1967). Know Your Cairn Terrier. New York: Pet Library. Accession No: OCLC: 2579232.
- Walin, D. (1983). The Cairn Terrier and West Highland White: Breed Standards, History, Care and Grooming. Oster Professional Products Department. Accession No: OCLC: 14081415.
- Whitehead, H. F. (edited & revised by Macdonald, A.) (1976; 1975). Cairn Terriers. New York: Arco Pub. ISBN 0668039671.
- Willis, J. R. (1993). Genetic Anomalies of the Cairn Terrier: A Reference Manual for Conscientious Breeders. Howell, MI: The Cairn Terrier Club of America. Accession No: OCLC: 41363972.

Scientific articles

- Gorke, B. ; Rentmeister, K. ; Peters, M. ; Siegert, F. ; Tipold, A. ; Hewicker-Trautwein, M. German. Title: Progressive neuronopathy in the Cairn terrier: two cases in Germany. Source: Wiener tierärztliche Monatsschrift. 88, Part 7 (2001): 183-186. Issue Id: Part 7. Alt Journal: Key Title: Wiener Tierärztliche Monatsschrift. Preceding Title: Tierärztliche zeitschrift. Succeeding Title: Deutsche tierharztliche Wochenschrift Berliner und Münchener tierärztliche Wochenschrift Tierärztliche rundschau Tierärztliche zeitschrift. Standard No: ISSN: 0043-535X CODEN: WTMOA3. OCLC No: 1696180. BL Shelfmark: 9316.000000
- Schaer, Michael ; Harvey, John W. ; Calderwood-Mays, Maron ; Giger, Urs. Title: Pyruvate Kinase Deficiency Causing Hemolytic Anemia with Secondary Hemochromatosis in a Cairn Terrier. Diagnosis is made from a liver biopsy and confirmed with electrophoretic and immunoprecipitation studies. Source: The Journal of the American Animal Hospital Association. 28, no. 3, (May 1992): 233-240. Alt Journal: Key Title: The Journal of the American Animal Hospital Association. Preceding Title: Animal hospital. Standard No: ISSN: 0587-2871 CODEN: JAAHBL
- Zaal, M D ; Ingh, T S G A M van den ; Goedegebuure, S & A ; Nes, J J van. Title: Progressive neuronopathy in two cairn terrier littermates; Source: The Veterinary quarterly. 19, no. 1, (1997): 34 (3 pages). Additional Info: Published for the Royal Netherlands Veterinary Association by Nijhoff.

Alt Journal: Key Title: The Veterinary quarterly. Preceding Title: Tijdschrift voor diergeneeskunde. Standard No: ISSN: 0165-2176 CODEN: VEQUDU. OCLC No: 5393794

External links

- Cairn Terrier coat color illustrations [5]
- A site for Cairn Terrier movie fans with film list & discriptions [6]
- A site for Cairn Terrier enthusiasts [7]
- Semi-Serious Q&A Based on Cairn Searches [8]

Clubs, associations, and societies

- Cairn Terrier Club of America [9]
- Cairn Terrier Club of Canada [10]
- Southern Cairn Terrier Club (UK) [11]
- Midland Cairn Terrier Club (UK) [12]
- North Ireland Cairn Terrier Club [13]
- Cairn Terrier Club of Norway [14]
- Cairn in Italy [15]
- Col Potter Cairn Rescue Network [16]
- Cairn Rescue League [17]
- Cairn Rescue USA [18]
- An Amusing Look at Cairn Terriers [19]
- Cairn Terrier Forum [20]
- Cairn Terrier Club of Southern California [21]

Dandie Dinmont Terrier

A **Dandie Dinmont Terrier** is a small breed of dog in the terrier family. The breed has a very long body, short legs, and a distinctive "top-knot" of hair on the head.

Description

Appearance

Originally bred to go to ground, the Dandie Dinmont Terrier is a long, low-stationed working terrier with a curved topline. The distinctive head with silken topknot is large but in proportion to the size of the dog. The dark eyes are large and round with a soft, wise expression. Dandie Dinmonts are between 8 and 11 inches tall at the top of the shoulders and can weigh between 18 and 24 pounds. The dogs are sturdily built with strong bone structure and ample muscular strength. The sturdy, flexible body and scimitar shaped tail are covered with a rather crisp double coat, either mustard or pepper in color. Pepper ranges from dark bluish black to a light silvery gray, the topknot is a silvery white. Mustard can range from a reddish brown to a pale fawn, with the topknot a creamy white.

This breed has little to no shedding. (see Moult)

Temperament

The Dandie Dinmont is affectionate and fun-loving. It makes a great companion dog. Lively, plucky, determined and willful. Independent and intelligent. Bold yet dignified. Reserved with strangers and protective of family and home. Good with all well-behaved children and babies as long as they are raised with them from puppyhood. Dominance level varies greatly. Some males can be aggressive with other male dogs in the household while females can be snappy and bad tempered

History

This short legged terrier was developed in the 17th century as an otter and badger specialist in the Cheviot and Teviotdale Hills in the border country of Scotland and England. The Dandie Dinmont Terrier is named after Dandie Dinmont, a jovial farmer in Sir Walter Scott's novel *Guy Mannering*. Scott also gave the names to the breed's colours, pepper and mustard, which were adopted from the names of Dandie Dinmont's dogs. The Dandie Dinmont Terrier is the only breed to be named after a character in fiction.

In the 1870s, exhibiting dogs became popular. The Kennel Club formed in 1873 and, just after this time, moves were made by Dandie enthusiasts to form a club. On November 17, 1875, at a meeting held at the Fleece Hotel in Selkirk on the Scottish Borders, the Dandie Dinmont Terrier Club [1] was formed. It is one of the oldest pedigree breed clubs in the world.

The first task was to draw up a breed standard and Mr William Wardlaw Reed, a founder member of the DDTC. worked on this, smoothing out the many differences. The following year at the Red Lion Hotel, Carlisle, the standard was agreed and adopted.

The breed was first registered with the American Kennel Club (AKC) in 1888. The Dandie Dinmont Terrier was recognized by the United Kennel Club (UKC) in 1918.

Today the Dandie Dinmont is amongst the rarest and most endangered of all pure breeds/pedigree dogs. The UK Kennel Club list the Dandie as one of the UK's Vulnerable Native Dog Breeds and there is a very real chance of the breed becoming extinct.

A Dandie Dinmont called Dodo features in Gerald Durrell's book: My Family and Other Animals Chapter 16.

External links

- The Caledonian Dandie Dinmont Terrier Club (UK) [2]
- The Dandie Dinmont Terrier Club (UK) [3]
- The Dandie Dinmont Terrier Club of America [4]
- The Dandie Dinmont Terrier Club of Canada [5]
- The Southern Dandie Dinmont Terrier Club (UK) [6]
- Dandie Dinmont Terriers in the UK [2]
- German Dandie information site [7]
- Dandie - gallery [8]
- Belgian Dandie information site [9]

Glen of Imaal Terrier

The **Glen of Imaal Terrier** is a breed of dog of the terrier category. It originates in the Glen of that name in Co. Wicklow, Ireland, and was developed as a working terrier, proficient in badger-drawing and hunting of fox. When Elizabeth I was having problems in Ireland she hired French and Hessian soldiers to go and solve the problem; they settled in the Wicklow area in the Glen of Imaal. They brought with them their low slung hounds which they bred with the Irish terrier stock developing the Glen of Imaal Terrier as a general working dog, used for herding and eradicating vermin, especially fox and badger.

Description

Appearance

The Glen of Imaal is classified as a medium-sized dog. When full grown, the average Glen of Imaal weighs approximately 16 kg (35 lbs) and stands 35.5 cm (14 in) tall at the withers. The breed has a medium-length double coat that is harsh on top and soft below. The coat is wheaten, blue, or brindle in colour. The breed also does not molt. Glens have a large head and short, bowed legs with a raised topline. Shoulders and chest are sturdy. The Glen of Imaal puppies have black highlights in their fur. Eventually, the black will fade and their full wheaten coat will come in. The breed is also slow to mature, taking up to four years; it goes through three growing stages before reaching maturity.

Health

Generally very strong and healthy, the breed can be prone to progressive retinal atrophy (a disease of the eyes) in a very small number of cases, and may possibly have heart problems (though there is only one recorded case). It is also a breed that requires a low protein diet after the age of twelve months.

Temperament

The Glen of Imaal Terrier, though normally docile, can sometimes be aggressive if provoked. There have been no reported serious injuries caused by the breed, but they are still a hunting terrier. This means that Glens have a high prey drive and might mistake domestic pets (cats, rats, gerbils, etc.) for prey. However, the Glen is highly intelligent and quite easily trained, so if properly trained and common sense is applied, this is generally not a problem. When hunting, they must work mute to ground as they are a strong dog, not a sounding terrier.

External links

- Glen of Imaal Terrier Club of America [1]
- GITCA breed standards [2]
- Independent Glen Rescue site [3]

Irish Terrier

The **Irish Terrier** is a dog breed from Ireland, one of many breeds of Terrier.

The Irish Terrier is an active and compactly sized dog that is suited for life in both rural and city environments. Its harsh red coat protects it from all kinds of weather.

Description

Appearance

Breed standards describe the ideal Irish Terrier as being racy, red and rectangular. Racy: an Irish Terrier should appear powerful without being sturdy or heavy. Rectangular: the outline of the Irish Terrier differs markedly from those of other terriers. The Irish Terrier's body is proportionately longer than that of the Fox Terrier, with a tendency toward racy lines but with no lack of substance.

The tail is customarily docked soon after birth to approximately two-thirds of the original length. In countries where docking is prohibited, the conformation judges emphasize tail carriage. The tail should start up quite high, but it should not stick straight up or curl over the back or either side. The ears are small and folded forward just above skull level. They are preferably slightly darker than the rest of the coat. It is fairly common to see wrongly positioned ears, even though most dogs have their ears trained during adolescence.

Coat and colour

The Irish Terrier is coloured golden red, red wheaten, or wheaten. Dark red is often mistaken as the only correct colour, possibly because wheaten coats are often of worse quality. As with many other solid-coloured breeds, a small patch of white is allowed on the chest. No white should appear elsewhere. As an Irish Terrier grows older, grey hair may appear here and there.

The outer part of the double coat should be straight and wiry in texture, never soft, silky, curly, wavy, or woolly as might be expected in the Kerry Blue Terrier. The coat should lie flat against the skin, and, though having some length, should never be so long as to hide the true shape of the dog. There are longer hairs on the legs, but never so much as a Wire Fox Terrier or Schnauzer. That means you have to have the coat trimmed often which can be expensive.

The inner part of the coat, called the under-wool or undercoat, should also be red. The under-wool may be hard for the inexperienced eye to see. Coat should be quite dense and so that "when parted with the fingers the skin is hardly visible".

A properly trimmed Irish Terrier should have some "furnishings" on legs and head. The slightly longer hair on the front legs should form even pillars, while the rear legs should only have some longer hair and not be trimmed too close to the skin. The chin is accentuated with a small beard. The beard should not be as profuse as that of a Schnauzer.

The eyes should be dark brown and quite small with a "fiery" expression. The eyes are topped with well-groomed eyebrows. The whole head should have good pigmentation.

Size

Most countries have breed descriptions that say that the Irish Terrier should not be more than 48 cm measured at the withers. However, it is not unusual to see bitches that are 50 cm tall or dogs that are even 53 cm (20 in). Younger generations are closer to the ideal, but there is a downside to this: when an Irish Terrier is very small and light-boned, it loses the correct racy type.

Very seldom does one see Irish Terriers that weigh only 11 to 12 kg (25-27 lb), as the original Kennel Club breed description states. 13 kg for a bitch and 15 for a dog are acceptable.

Temperament

The Irish Terrier is full of life, but not hyperactive; it should be able to relax inside the house and be roused to full activity level quickly.

Irish Terriers are good with people. Most Irish Terriers love children and tolerate rough-housing to a certain extent. Irish terriers are not always the best choice of dog, as they are very energetic and sometimes challenging to train. It is important that they have a strong leader, for whom they have natural respect. New tasks are easily mastered, providing the dog is motivated to learn; Irish terriers have less of an eagerness to please people than some other breed. In motivating, food and toys work equally well. Training will not be as easy as with other dog breeds that have stronger willingness to please people. They respond best to firm, consistent training from a relaxed, authoritative person. As with all dog breeds, violence should never be used - it is always best to outwit and lure. When seeking a trainer, one should look for a person who has experience with terriers.

Irish Terriers are often dominant with other dogs, and same-sex aggression is a common problem. The Irish Terrier will commonly be attracted to species of the same-sex. Poorly socialized individuals can start fights with minimal, if any, provocation. Thus, early socialization is a necessity. Most have strong guarding instincts and when these instincts are controlled, make excellent alarming watchdogs, but if they are not controlled, your dog will be very aggressive and not very compassionate towards the owner.

Most Irish Terriers are show dogs. There are however more and more people joining organised dog sports with their terriers. The obedience training required at a certain level in most dog sports is fairly easy, though the precision and long-lasting drive needed in the higher levels may be hard to achieve. Many Irish Terriers excel in agility, even though it may be hard to balance the speed, independence and precision needed in the higher levels. To date there is one Agility Champion in the US, and a handful of Finnish and Swedish Irish terriers compete at the most difficult classes.

Irish Terriers have a good nose and can learn to track either animal blood or human scent. Many Irish Terriers enjoy Lure Coursing, although they are not eligible for competition like sight hounds are. In Finland one Irish Terrier is a qualified Rescue Dog specializing at Sea Rescue.

History

The breed's origin is not known. It is believed to have descended from the black and tan terrier-type dogs of Britain and Ireland, just like the Kerry Blue and Irish Soft-haired Wheaten Terriers in Ireland or the Welsh, Lakeland and Scottish Terriers in Great Britain.

F. M. Jowett writes in *The Irish Terrier*, 'Our Dogs' Publishing Co. Ltd., Manchester, England 1947 - 7th Edition: They are described by an old Irish writer as being the poor man's sentinel, the farmer's friend, and the gentleman's favourite...These dogs were originally bred not so much for their looks as for their working qualities and gameness, the Irish Terrier being by instinct a thorough vermin killer. They were formerly of all types and of all colours - black-and-tan, grey-and-brindle, wheaten of all shades, and red being the predominant colours. Colour or size evidently did not matter if they were hardy and game."

The proper selection process of the breed began only in the latter 19th century. They were shown now and then, sometimes in one class, sometimes in separate classes for dogs under and over 9 pounds.

The first breed club was set up in Dublin in 1879. Irish Terriers were the first members of the terrier group to be recognized by the English Kennel Club as a native Irish Breed - this happened just before the end of the 19th century. The first Irish Terriers were taken to the US in the late 19th century and quickly became somewhat popular.

Although the breed has never been very "fashionable", there used to be big influential kennels in Ireland, the Great Britain and US up to the 1960s. Nowadays there is ambitious breeding in many continents, including Africa (South Africa), North America, (Northern) Europe and Australia.

Care

When groomed properly, the Irish Terrier coat will protect the dog from rain and cold. A properly cared-for Irish Terrier does not shed either. The wiry coat is fairly easy to groom, pet dogs (rather than show dogs) needing stripping only once or twice a year.

The coat must be stripped by hand or a non-cutting knife to retain its weather-resistant qualities. This does not hurt the dog when done properly. Keeping the skin above the stripped section taut with the other hand helps especially where the skin is looser, i.e. belly and chest. Never cut the coat - use your fingers or a non-cutting knife. If the coat is clipped, it loses colour and becomes softer, thus losing its weather-resistant characteristics. For the same reason the coat should not be washed too often, as detergents take away the natural skin oils. Most Irish terriers only need washing when dirty.

When stripping, the coat may be "taken down" entirely to leave the dog in the undercoat until a new coat grows in. For a pet, this should be done at least twice a year. When a show-quality coat is required, it can be achieved in many ways. One is by "rolling the coat", i.e. stripping the dog every X weeks to remove any dead hair. Before a show an expert trimmer is needed to mould especially the head and legs.

Most Irish Terriers need to have their ears trained during adolescence. Otherwise the ears may stick up, roll back or hang down unaesthetically.

Health

Irish Terrier is a generally healthy breed. The life expectancy is around 13 − 14 years.

The proportions are not over-exaggerated in any way and thus eye or breathing problems are rare. Most Irish Terriers do not show signs of allergies towards foods. As they are small dogs, the breed has a very low incidence of hip dysplasia.

In the 1960s and 1970s there were problems with hyperkeratosis, a disease causing corny pads and severe pain. Today it is widely known which dogs carried the disease and respectable breeders do not use those bloodlines any more. A health study conducted by the Irish Terrier Club of America showed a greater-than-expected incidence of hypothyroidism and cataracts. There are not enough eye-checked individuals to draw any conclusions.

Appearances in arts and culture

Irish Terriers have appeared in the arts every now and then.

Jack London's books *Jerry of the Islands* and *Michael, Brother of Jerry* were about Irish Terriers, that according to the bloodlines recorded in the beginning of the book may actually have lived.

It is said that Disney's Tramp in 'Lady and the Tramp', although a mutt, was drawn to resemble an Irish Terrier. (In the comic book versions the brownish red color of Tramp has been changed to grey.)

The 2007 film *Firehouse Dog* features an Irish Terrier as the title character.

Former Canadian Prime Minister William Lyon Mackenzie King owned several Irish Terriers (all named Pat), and had séances to "communicate" with the first Pat after the dog's death.

Alexandra Day's children's picture book Paddy's Payday features an Irish Terrier as the title character. (Day is best known for her book Good Dog, Carl.)

External links

- Irish Terriers Community [1]
- Irish Terrier Association of Canada [2]
- Irish Terrier Club of America [3]
- Irish Terrier Association (U.K) [4]
- Finnish Irish Terrier Association [5]

Kerry Blue Terrier

The **Kerry Blue Terrier** is a breed of dog mistakenly thought to be of County Kerry in South West Ireland; it is actually from Tipperary. In its motherland it is often called the Irish Blue Terrier. Over time the Kerry became a general working dog used for a variety of jobs, including herding cattle and sheep and as a guard dog. It was, however, primarily developed for controlling "vermin" including rats, rabbits, badgers, foxes, otters and hares. Today the Kerry has spread around the world as a companion and working dog. Despite a Kerry Blue winning Crufts - the most important UK dog show - in 2000, it remains an uncommon breed. Not as threatened as some of the other terrier breeds (Skye Terrier, Sealyham Terrier, Dandie Dinmont Terrier), it is still distinctly uncommon.

Description

Appearance

Some characteristics of the Kerry Blue Terrier include a long head, flat skull, deep chest, and a soft wavy to curly coat that comes in several shades of blue (from blue-black to light slate grey). The coat is considered to have more "color" or to be more "blue" when it carries more of the grey/blue color (or the lighter the coat is). Puppies are born black; the blue appears gradually as the puppy grows older, usually up to 2 years of age. All kennel clubs have statements in their standard similar to that of the American Kennel Club: "Black on the muzzle, head, ears, tail and feet is permissible at any age." This indicates the presence of the melanistic mask gene. The ideal Kerry should be 18-1/2 inches at the withers for a male, slightly less for the female. The most desirable weight for a fully developed male is from 33-40 pounds, females weighing proportionately less.

Coat

The coat is the key feature of the Kerry. It is soft and wavy with no undercoat. The texture is similar to that of fine human hair and like human hair is not shed but continues to grow throughout the year. This means the Kerry Blue requires very regular grooming (at least once per week) and clipping an average of every 6 weeks. as they don't lose their hair, your house stays much cleaner. You will not find hairs in your house from a Kerry.

Temperament

Kerry Blue Terriers are strong-headed and highly spirited. They have always been loyal and affectionate towards their owners and very gentle towards children. In the early days of competitive dog showing the Irish Kennel Club required Kerries to pass a "gameness" test, known as Teastas Mor certification, before they were deemed worthy of being judged. These tests included catching rabbits and bringing a badger to bay in its set. They are fast, strong, and intelligent. They do well in obedience, dog agility, sheep herding, and tracking. They have been used as police dogs in Ireland. Modern breeders have attempted to retain high spirits whilst breeding out aggression.

As a long-legged breed, the activity level of the Kerry Blue Terrier ranges from moderate to high. They require an active, skilled owner who can provide them with early socialization and obedience training. Kerries require daily exercise.

Health

Kerries are fairly healthy, however there are some genetic disorders that are prevalent in the breed. They are prone to eye problems such as keratoconjunctivitis sicca (dry eyes), cataracts, and entropion. They sometimes get cysts or cancerous growths in their skin, but these are rarely malignant. Hip dysplasia, hypothyroidism, and cryptorchidism have also been reported. Another skin-related health issue is spiculosis. This is a skin disorder that produces abnormally thick hairs that are also called thorns, spikes, or bristles.

Progressive neuronal abiotrophy [1] (PNA) is also seen. This condition is also referred to as canine multiple system degeneration (CMSD), cerebellar cortical abiotrophy (CCA) or cerebellar abiotrophy (CA). This is a progressive movement disorder that begins with cerebellar ataxia [2] between 10 and 14 weeks of age. After 6 months of age, affected dogs develop difficulty initiating movements and fall frequently. The gene responsible has been mapped to canine chromosome 1.

History

The Kerry Blue terrier was first observed in the mountains of County Kerry in Ireland, hence the name of the breed. There is a romantic story of a blue dog swimming ashore from a shipwreck: the coat of this dog was so lovely that it was mated with all the female Wheaten Terriers in Kerry (or in all Ireland according to some), producing the Kerry Blue. Perhaps this story is not entirely myth as the Portuguese Water Dog is often suggested as part of the Kerry's make up. Others suggest the Kerry was produced by the Soft Coated Wheaten Terrier crossed with the Bedlington Terrier with (or without) some Irish Wolfhound or Irish Terrier blood. The extinct Gadhar herding dog is also mentioned as another possible branch of the Kerry's family tree. One certain fact is the breed became very popular as an all-around farm dog in rural Ireland.

National Dog of Ireland

With the development of dog shows in the late 19th and early 20th century the breed became standardised and tidied up for the show ring. It was closely associated with Irish nationalism with the nationalist leader Michael Collins owning a famous Kerry Blue named Convict 225. Indeed Collins made an attempt to have the Kerry Blue adopted as the national dog of Ireland.

It should be stated, however, that the love of dogs crossed political divides. The first show of the Dublin Irish Blue Terrier club took place outside official curfew hours and was entered by those fighting for and against an Ireland Republic. The Dublin Irish Blue Terrier Club was so successful it led directly to the foundation of the Irish Kennel Club. A Kerry Blue was the first dog registered with the Irish Kennel Club.

Famous Owners

At Crufts in 2008 a number of celebrities were named as owners of Kerry Blue Terriers. These included:

- Henry Cooper (boxer) (Heavyweight Boxer)
- Jack Dempsey (Heavyweight Boxer)
- Gene Tunney (Heavyweight Boxer)
- Perry Como (Entertainer)
- Alfred Hitchcock (Film Director)
- Michael Mann (Film Director)
- Jeremy Schoemaker (Web Entrepreneur)

See also

- Badger-baiting - Kerries were once used for this sport.

External links

- United States Kerry Blue Terrier Club [3]
- Kerry Blue Terrier breed info [4]
- Kerry Blue Terrier Club of Southern California [5] since 1946.
- The Kerry Blue Terrier Foundation [6]
- Irish Kennel Club [7]
- Dublin Irish Blue Terrier Club [8]

Lakeland Terrier

The **Lakeland Terrier** is a dog breed, one of many Terrier breeds, that originated in the Lake District of England as a descendant of the old English Black and Tan and Fell Terriers for the purpose of hunting vermin.

The Lakeland Terrier originated in the Lake District of Cumberland, England near the Scottish border in the 1800s. He is related to several terrier breeds and is one of the oldest working terrier breeds still in use today. His diverse ancestors include the now extinct Old English Black and Tan terrier, the early Dandie Dinmont Terrier, Bedlington Terrier and Border Terrier.

For generations, the Lakeland has been used in the Lake District for the purpose of exterminating the fell foxes which raid the farmer's sheep fold during the lambing season. Whereas most terrier breeds have only to bolt their quarry, or to mark it by baying, the Lakeland must be able to kill the foxes in their lair. Despite his reputation for courage and tenacity, the Lakeland is a gentle and loving companion.

Description

Appearance

The Lakeland is similar to the Welsh Terrier being slightly shorter and considerably finer-boned. Grizzle Lakelands are often mistaken as "Miniature Airdales". This breed has thick, hard wiry outer coat and a soft undercoat. The Lakeland comes in 10 colors which are black and tan, blue and tan, liver and tan, tan grizzle, red, red grizzle, wheaten, liver, blue, or black. They have an upright tail. Lakeland Terriers grow to between 33 and 38 cm (13 to 14.5 inches) in height measured to the withers with a weight of between 7 and 8 kg (16 to 17 lbs). They are known for their minimal shedding of hair.

The eyes are small and dark colored. The nose and pads of the feet are black except in liver colored dogs where the nose and pad coloring will be liver colored.

This breed has little to no shedding (see Moult).

Temperament

The dogs are friendly, bold, and confident. Shyness is very atypical, as is aggressiveness. Intelligent and independent minded, especially when going after prey, they are quick to learn and easy to train, though Lakelands seem to exhibit 'selective deafness' when their interest level is aroused. They are not "yappy," barking only when they have reason.

History

In 1925 the breed attained homogeneity following a cross-breeding with the Fox Terrier and the Airedale Terrier. The Lakeland Terrier is suitable for fox hunting and rabbit hunting, and are especially talented hunters of vermin.

In the Lake District of the UK, the mountainous, rocky terrain is unsuitable for hunting fox on horseback and foxes were hunted on foot. It has been suggested that the lakeland terrier's great stamina derives from running all day with the hounds, unlike his close cousin, the fox terrier, who would have been carried in a saddle bag to be released only when the fox had gone to earth.

The working dog version of the Lakeland is often known as the Fell Terrier or Patterdale Terrier.

Famous Lakelands

- Zelda Van Gutters- Nickelodeon Magazine's Roving Reporter/Mascot
- Champion Revelry's Awesome Blossom - Top winning Lakeland Terrier in the history of the breed. Owned by Jean L. Heath and Bill Cosby.
- Stingray of Derrybah - the first dog to win Best in Show/Supreme Champion at both the top US and UK shows (Westminster and Crufts). (1967)
- Kevin, owned by Neil Tennant (Singer of the Pet Shop Boys). Pictures: [1][2]

External links

- United States Lakeland Terrier Club, Inc. [3]
- The Lakeland Terrier Club (UK) [4]
- Terrier Network - Show, Field and Hunt [5]

Manchester Terrier

The **Manchester Terrier** is a breed of dog of the smooth-haired terrier type.

Appearance

Manchester Terriers are considered by most to be the oldest of all identifiable terrier breeds, finding mention in works dating from as early as the 16th century. In 1570 Dr. Caius (*Encyclopedia of Dogs*) gives mention to the 'Black and Tan Terrier,' though he referred to a rougher coated, shorter legged dog than we are now accustomed to.

By the early 1800s a closer facsimile to the current Manchester Terrier had evolved. In *The Dog in Health and Disease* by J. A. Walsh a full chapter was devoted to the Black and Tan, for the first time recognizing it as an established breed. The description Walsh set forth might, in fact, serve well today: Smooth haired, long tapering nose, narrow flat skull, eyes small and bright, chest rather deep than wide, only true color black and tan.

This breed has maintained consistency in type and appearance for nearly two centuries (at the very least).

Varieties

In its native England, the Kennel Club (UK) recognizes the Manchester Terrier in the Terrier Group and the closely related English Toy Terrier (Black and Tan) in the Toy Group.

In North America the Manchester Terrier is divided into two varieties. The Toy Manchester Terrier was originally recognized as a separate breed in 1938, bred down in size from the Manchester Terrier. The Toy Manchester Terrier weighs less than 12 pounds and has naturally erect ears, never cropped. It is placed in the Toy Group by the Canadian Kennel Club and the American Kennel Club, although the Manchester Terrier is placed in the Terrier Group. The Manchester Terrier non-toy variety weighs 12 to 22 pounds and has 3 allowable ear types (naturally erect, button, or cropped). Other than size differences and ear type, the Manchester Terrier and the Toy Manchester Terrier have the same over all appearance, and since 1958 have been varieties of the same breed.

History

The following is a brief overview of the breed's history in both its native England and America:

In England

The early 1800s saw times of poor sanitation in England. Rats soon became a health menace and rat killing became a popular sport. John Hulme, enthusiastic devotee of the sport of rat killing and rabbit coursing, crossed a Whippet to a cross bred terrier to produce a tenacious, streamlined animal infinitely suited to the sport. (Perhaps the Whippet influence explains the unusual topline of the Manchester still required today). This cross proved so successful that it was repeated, resulting in the establishment of a definite type—thus the Manchester Terrier was born.

By 1827 the breed's fighting spirit had made it equally handy along a hedge row as in a rat-pit. The Manchester could tackle, with silent determination, an opponent twice its size. Ears were cropped to save risk of being torn in frequent scraps. (This also enhanced the sharp appearance of the expression). When rat-killing became illegal in England rat-pits were supplanted by dining halls or public inns, all of which were infested by rats. To combat the rodent problem each inn kept kennels. When the taprooms closed, who do you think took command? The little Black and Tan rat killers who proved their worth one hundredfold to the inn keeper.

1860 saw the city of Manchester in England as the breed centre for these "Rat Terriers" and the name Manchester Terrier surfaced. Smaller specimens began to gain appeal. Unethical persons were known to introduce Chihuahuas in order to reduce size to as small as 2½ pounds. This resulted in numerous problems, including apple heads, thinning coats, and poppy eyes. Inbreeding further diminished size yet the smaller versions, though delicate and sickly, remained popular for some time.

Smaller Manchesters were carried in specially designed leather pouches suspended from the rider's belt, (earning the title of "Groom's Pocket Piece"). With their smaller stature these dogs obviously could not keep up with the hounds, but when the hounds ran the fox into dense thickets they were not able to penetrate, the little Manchester Terrier was released. Nicknamed the "Gentleman's Terrier" this breed was never a "sissy." His dauntless spirit commanded respect.

In the United States

As in its native country the Manchester gained quick acceptance as a recognized breed. In 1886, just two years after the American Kennel Club was organized, the first Black and Tan Terrier was registered in the stud book. The following year "Lever" (AKC #7585) became the first AKC recognized Manchester Terrier.

The 20th century is dotted by the recognition of breed clubs devoted to preserving and promoting this breed:

In 1923 the "Manchester Terrier Club of America" was recognized and 1934 saw the Toy Black and Tan Terrier changed to Toy Manchester Terrier, and in 1938 the "American Toy Manchester Terrier Club" was recognized.

By 1952, however, the "Manchester Terrier Club of America" (Standards) was without organized breed representation. To the credit of the "American Toy Manchester Terrier Club", the two breeds were combined as one (with two varieties - Standard and Toy) with the formation of the "American Manchester Terrier Club" in 1958, an organization which still survives today.

See also

* Rat-baiting
* Toy Manchester Terrier
* English Toy Terrier (Black and Tan)

External links

* Breed clubs
  * Canadian Manchester Terrier Club [1]
  * American Manchester Terrier Club [2]
  * British Manchester Terrier Club [3]
* Information
  * Terriers at rat pits [4]
  * Manchester Terrier Pedigree Database [5]

Bull Terrier (Miniature)

The **Bull Terrier (Miniature)** is a breed with origins in the English White Terrier, the Dalmatian and the Bulldog. The first existence is documented 1872 in *The Dogs of British Island*.

Description

Appearance

Miniature Bull Terriers have short, fine, and glossy coats that are very close to the skin, like the Bull Terriers. They are accepted in the ring to be white, white with another color, or fully colored. However, like the Standards, any blue or liver colored coats are undesirable. These dogs require very minimal grooming.

In the early 1900s, the difference between the breeds was determined by the dog's weight. However, this led to Miniature Bull Terriers becoming so small and fine that they looked more like a Chihuahua than a Bull Terrier. So, in the 1970s, the weight limit was replaced with a height limit of under fourteen inches. They are usually no smaller than ten inches. According to the AKC, miniature bull terriers weight must be proportionate to its height. However, they tend to range anywhere from 20–35 lbs.

The Miniature Bull Terriers have a very strong build. They have very muscular shoulders and a full body.

Miniature Bull Terriers, like the Bull Terrier, have a head described as "egg-shaped." It is flat on top with a Roman muzzle. The eyes are triangular and closely set.

The ears are carried erect and are not cropped or otherwise altered.

The tail is carried horizontally rather than vertically.

Temperament

Like the Bull Terriers, Minis are loving and, like many terrier breeds, can be stubborn at times; but despite this they make great dogs for people with limited space.

Miniature Bull Terriers are known to be stubborn and courageous. They don't seem to realize their size, however, because even if confronting an enormous dog they will not back down. However, with the right training, confrontations can be avoided. They are very energetic and playful. They love people, but often don't get along with other pets. They are variable around other dogs, and young children must be warned to treat them carefully.

Care

As mentioned before, Miniature Bull Terriers require little grooming. A quick brushing once a day or a few times a week is sufficient to keep the fur in order, as it cannot become tangled due to its length. Sunscreen must be used on any sparse white sections of fur around the face, ears, hindquarters or stomach when outdoors (especially in the summer between the hours of 10am and 2pm) to avoid sunburn and cancer.

Training

Miniatures do require a lot of training, particularly early on. They must be heavily socialized and trained to obey early in their lives.

They also are very energetic and seem to be able to play endlessly as puppies. However, as they grow older they become less energetic. They must be carefully exercised and dieted to avoid obesity.

Health

Miniature Bull Terriers are generally quite healthy, but there are hearing, eye, skin, kidney, heart and knee problems in some dogs:

Deafness occurs in both coloured and white Bull Terrier (Miniature). Puppies can be born unilaterally deaf (deaf in one ear) or bilaterally (deaf in both ears.) Deaf dogs should not be bred due to deafness being hereditary. BEAP (or BAER) testing is done on puppies prior to sale to discover which puppies have hearing problems.

Bull Terrier (Miniature) are also susceptible to having luxating patellas. This is a knee problem common in small dogs. It can be treated by surgery.

Polycystic kidney disease (PKD) and Bull Terrier hereditary nephritis (BTHN) are autosomal dominant diseases. PKD is diagnosed by Ultrasonic scan by a specialist veterinarian. BTHN is diagnosed by a UPC test. Dogs with a score of .3 or below are considered clear of the disease. Clearing breeding stock prior to use ensures that progeny are not affected with the disease.

Miniature Bull Terriers are also susceptible to eye problems such as primary lens luxation. PLL is a late onset disease which typically affects dogs between the ages of 3 and 7. Younger and older cases are known. During September 2009 a definitive DNA test was released by the Animal Health Trust. This test gives three results: Clear, Carrier, Affected.

Aortic valve stenosis and mitral valve dysplasia are heart diseases. Diagnosis is made by colour doppler echocardiography scanning by a specialist veterinarian.

The skin of a Miniature can be a problem. Pyotraumatic dermatitis (hot spots), allergic reactions, and hives can be problematic. This is typically due to feeding a processed diet high in grains. Breeders with experience find that changing the dogs diet to unprocessed raw foods eliminates skin problems in the breed.

History

When the Standard breed was first created in 19th century England, it was about the same size as Miniature Bull Terriers. Crossbreeding with Pointers increased the size so it was an optimal fighting size. Miniature Bull Terriers were granted membership in the American Kennel Club (AKC) in May 14, 1991 (effective January 1, 1992).

Interbreeding

Interbreeding, the process of mating together a Bull Terrier (Miniature) and Bull Terrier, is allowed, only for a short time, in Australia, New Zealand, and the United Kingdom. Interbreeding is undertaken to reduce the incidence of Primary Lens Luxation in the Miniature. The Bull Terrier does not carry the PLL gene so all progeny are phenotypically normal for the disease.

Each country which allows interbreding have their own protocols which govern which dogs can be mated. Australia has no protocols, while the United Kingdom and New Zealand requires strict adherence to health testing and identification of dogs used.

External links

- The Miniature Bull Terrier Club of America [1]
- Onion - Celebrity Miniature Bull Terrier! [2]

See also

- Bull Terrier

Miniature Schnauzer

The **Miniature Schnauzer** is a breed of small dog of the Schnauzer type that originated in Germany in the mid-to-late 19th century. Miniature Schnauzers developed from crosses between the Standard Schnauzer and one or more smaller breeds such as the Poodle and Affenpinscher.

The breed remains one of the most popular world wide, primarily for its temperament and relatively small size. Globally, the Miniature Schnauzer comes in four colors: black, salt-and-pepper, black-and-silver, and white. As of 2008 it is the 11th most popular breed in the U.S,, though the American Kennel Club recognizes only three colors and considers solid white a disqualification.. Colors such as chocolate, liver, and parti (multi-color or spotted) are available on the pet trade and can be registered as pure-breds by some organizations, but are not currently recognized by any legitimate clubs for conformation shows.

Appearance

Miniature Schnauzers normally have a small, squarely proportioned build, measuring tall and weighing for females and for males. They have a double coat. The exterior fur is wiry and the undercoat is softer. The coat is trimmed short on the body, but the hair on ears, legs, and edge of the body, a.k.a. the "furnishings", are retained. The first Breed Standard for the Schnauzer, established in 1907, required specific color formation: "Color: All salt and pepper color shades or similar bristly equal color mixtures and solid black. Faults: ...All white, speckled, brindles, red, or bran colors."

Miniature Schnauzers are often described as non-shedding dogs, and while this is not entirely true, their shedding is minimal and generally unnoticeable. They are characterized by a long head with bushy beard, mustache and eyebrows; teeth that meet in a "scissor bite"; oval and dark colored eyes; and v-shaped, natural forward-folding ears. (When cropped, the ears point straight upward and come to a sharp point.) Their tails are naturally thin and short, and may be docked (where permitted). They will also have very straight, rigid front legs, and feet that are short and round (so-called "cat feet") with thick, black pads.

Temperament

The Official Standard of the Miniature Schnauzer describes temperament as "alert and spirited, yet obedient to command. He is friendly, intelligent and willing to please. He should never be overaggressive or timid." Usually easy to train, they tend to be excellent watchdogs, with a good territorial instinct, but more inclined toward vocal notification than attack. They are often guarded towards strangers until the owners of the home welcome the guest, upon which they are typically very friendly to them; unlike some of their terrier cousins, they are not typically aggressive. However, they will express themselves vocally, and may bark to greet their owner, or to express joy, excitement, or displeasure.

Proper socialization with other dogs and people is important. The breed is generally good with children, but as with any dog, play with small children should be supervised. They are highly playful dogs, and if not given the outlet required for their energy they can become bored and invent their own "fun." Schnauzers have a "high prey drive" (appropriate for a ratting dog), which means they may attack other small pets such as birds, snakes, and rodents. Many will also attack cats, but this may be curbed with training, or if the dog is raised with cats.

History

The earliest records surrounding development of the Standard Schnauzer (or Mittleschnauzer) in Germany come from the late 1800s. They were originally bred to be medium-sized farm dogs in Germany, equally suited to ratting, herding, and guarding property and children. As time passed, farmers bred down the Standard Schnauzer into a smaller, more compact size perfect for ratting around the house and barn.

Several small breeds were employed in crosses to bring down the size of the well-established Standard Schnauzer, with the goal of creating a duplicate in miniature. Crossing to other breeds, such as the Affenpinscher and Poodle, had the side effect of introducing colors that were not considered acceptable to the ultimate goal — and as breeders worked towards the stabilization of the gene pool, miss-marked particolors (mixed colors) and white puppies were removed from breeding programs. Since the 1950s, white puppies have re-emerged as a potential color variant, giving rise to the White Schnauzer Controversy of North America (see below).

Recognition

The first recorded Miniature Schnauzer appeared in 1888, and the first exhibition was held in 1899. The AKC accepted registration of the new breed in 1926, two years after Miniature Schnauzers were introduced to the United States. The AKC groups this breed with the Terriers, because it was developed for a similar purpose and has a similar character to the terrier breeds of the Britain and Ireland. Though the Miniature Schnauzer was bred to be a ratter like the British terriers, it is more correctly termed a Pinscher (a descriptive word like Setter or Retriever).

The Miniature Schnauzer was recognized by the United Kennel Club in 1948 and also groups the breed as a terrier. The United Kingdom The Kennel Club however, does not accept the Miniature Schnauzer as a true Terrier because it does not originate from the terrier breeds of the British Isles. Like the Tibetan Terrier and Boston Terrier, it lists the Miniature Schnauzer in the Utility group for shows run under the UK Kennel Club rules such as Crufts.

The World Canine Organization accepts the Schnauzer breeds but, again, does not list the Miniature Schnauzer as a Terrier, although it accepts the White Schnauzer for conformation.

Health and grooming

While generally a healthy breed, Miniature Schnauzers may suffer health problems associated with high fat levels. Such problems include hyperlipidemia, which may increase the possibility of pancreatitis, though either may form independently. Other issues which may affect this breed are diabetes, bladder stones and eye problems. Feeding the dog low- or non-fatty and unsweetened foods may help avoid these problems. Miniature Schnauzers are also prone to *comedone syndrome*, a condition that produces pus filled bumps, usually on their backs, which can be treated with a variety of protocols. Miniature Schnauzers should have their ears dried after swimming due to a risk of infection, especially those with uncropped ears; ear examinations should be part of the regular annual check up.

Schnauzers require regular grooming, either by stripping (mostly seen in show dogs), or by clipping (a short-cut usually reserved for family pets). Stripping removes the loose, dead coat; it may be done by hand, called finger stripping, or plucking, or with a stripping knife; either way, it is a laborious process. Many Miniature Schnauzers who are family pets have regular grooming appointments to have their hair clipped; clipping, using a mechanical clippers (or shaver), produces a soft, silky, skin-close trim. Whether stripped or clipped, the coat is close at the body, and falls into a fringe-like foundation on their undercarriage, called furnishings, which can be left to grow, but must be combed regularly. All Schnauzers, whether they are minis, Standards, or Giants, often sport a beard, created by allowing the hair around their noses to grow out. Left unclipped or unstripped, the body hair will grow two to four inches, and will often tangle into mats and curls.

White Schnauzer Controversy of North America

The White Schnauzer is one of four color varieties of the Miniature Schnauzer recognized by the Pinscher-Schnauzer Klub of Germany and the World Canine Organization. Not all dog fanciers accept the white variety as a legitimate variation for conformation (show) standards and they are not accepted by either the American Kennel Club or the Canadian Kennel Club. The controversy rests on the disputed origins of the white variation, if it is a naturally occurring, albeit recessive, color, an albino characteristic, or an unhealthy genetic mutation.

From pedigree research, the "white" (*gelb* or "yellow" as it was called in early German records) gene was introduced into the Miniature Schnauzer breed mainly through a German black Champion Miniature Schnauzer named Peter V Westerberg (PZ604), born in November 1902. Peter was obviously carrying one "e" gene because it is recorded that he was bred to a female named Gretel VD Werneburg (PZ1530) (color unknown) and produced a "yellow" female pup named Mucki VD Werneburg (PSZ 8) born October 1914. Mucki was bred to a grandson of Peter named Pucki VD Werneburg, a dark Salt and Pepper variation PSZ12, who in turn produced the black German Champion Peterle VD Werneburg, PSZ11 born June 2, 1916, who also had to have the "e" gene, since his dam was yellow. Peter V Westerburg or his grandson, *Peterle* (literally, little Peter), can be traced to nearly every Miniature Schnauzer line researched in AKC records. For example, tracing every ancestor in the 5th generation of Dorem Display reveals every dog goes back to Peter Von Westerberg. Any time one established breed is crossed with another, or when breeds are bred over generations for specific features, for whatever reason, part of that breed's characteristics are inherited through the DNA structure, whether it be color, structure, working ability, temperament, disease, or any other heritable trait. The only way to prove whether a dog carries a certain inherited breed trait is by DNA testing, and DNA testing was not available when white first appeared as a coat color in miniature Schnauzers. Miniature Schnauzer breeders claimed they had eradicated the white gene in the early twentieth century. With so many line-bred crosses, it is statistically impossible to eradicate the "white" "e" gene by visual assessment alone.

Compounding the controversy, there are no known factual data to back up the assertion that *gelb* is equal to 'white'. The originators of the breed in the late 1800s and early 1900s in Germany wanted an exact duplicate of the Standard Schnauzer. The Standard Schnauzer has never appeared in the white or even the *gelb* color variety. The original Schnauzer Club in Germany disqualified whites and told breeders of Parti colors and solid whites to not continue to produce those colors, as they went against the ideal breed standard.

Coat color inheritance

After testing several unrelated white dogs from around the world, it has been recently proven by DNA testing that the genotype for the White Miniature Schnauzer is "e/e" at MC1r (commonly referred to as the "E" locus). The "E", a normal extension of black, allows the A-series alleles to show through, and "e", recessive red/yellow, overrides whatever gene is present at the A locus to produce a dog which shows only phaeomelanin pigment in the coat. Skin and eye color show apparently normal eumelanin, although some "e,e" dogs appear to show reduced pigment on the nose, especially in winter (snow nose), but after sunbathing in warm weather, they regain the dark brown pigment on their noses, much like humans getting a tan in summer. Most white Miniature Schnauzers with original harsh coats will have a yellowish streak on their backs and head when their hair is hand stripped and the ends become blown or dead. It is assumed this is why they were originally called "yellow" in German records.

There are two forms of melanin (pigment) in mammals' hair coats. The first is called *eumelanin*. The base form of eumelanin is black. Eumelanin can also appear brown (often called liver in dogs) or blue-gray. The second pigment, which varies from pale cream through shades of yellow, tan, and orange/red is called *phaeomelanin*.

All dogs have alleles at every locus. Not all proposed alleles have been proven to exist. The generally recognized color loci in dogs are referred to as: A (agouti), B (brown), C (albino series), D (blue dilution) E (extension), G (graying), M (merle), R (roaning), S (white spotting) and T (ticking.) There may be more, still unrecognized gene series, and in a given breed, modifying factors may drastically affect the actual appearance. The newest proposed locus is the K locus for dominant black in certain breeds, including the Miniature Schnauzer.

White Miniature Schnauzers do not possess the "d" allele, which is commonly known as the Dilution gene responsible for diluting both eumelanin and phaeomelanin pigment. This stands to reason because true white Miniature Schnauzers have black skin pigment and dark eyes.

Genotypes for the white Miniature Schnauzer are proposed as follows, showing they can "carry" for any of the other three colors of solid Black, B&S or S&P.

aw,aw	D,D	e,e	k,k (white carrying for S&P)
aw,at	D,D	e,e	K,k (white carrying for S&P, B&S, and black)
at,at	D,D	e,e	K,k (white carrying for B&S, and black)

This "e,e" genotype for the white Miniature Schnauzer proves that all of the other 3 colors can carry a gene for the white and also that any of the three colored schnauzers bred to another schnauzer of any color that is carrying one "e" gene can produce a white puppy from that mating.

Therefore, a B&S with the genotype of at,at; E,e; K,k bred to another B&S with the same genotype *can* produce a white puppy. The statistical odds are:

* 50% will be: at,at; E,e; K,k, (B&S)
* 25% will be: at,at; E,E,; K,k (B&S)
* 25% will be: at,at; e,e; K,k (white)

Mating 2 white miniature Schnauzers together will produce 100% white puppies because white is a double recessive gene phenotype.

Controversy today

Today, the American Miniature Schnauzer Club and the American Kennel Club standard describes the White Miniature Schnauzers as a disqualification from conformation shows. The American Miniature Schnauzer Club and AKC maintain the colors from original breed standards. Breeders of the white variant claim that these dogs have no known congenital or lethal white gene theories. They are not albino dogs, and white dogs described as Miniature Schnauzers are affectionate and robust dogs who exhibit all the qualities of their colored counterparts. The Federation Cynologique Internationale (FCI) now acknowledges white in the breed standards set forth by the countries of breed origins. The White Miniature Schnauzer may compete in other AKC sanctioned events such as agility, Canine Good Citizen, Obedience, or Earthdog trials, but not in conformation competition. The White Miniature Schnauzer may be shown in Conformations shows sanctioned by the FCI in international competitions, and the white variant is becoming very popular in Europe as a show dog.

The White Miniature Schnauzer Initiative was established in 2006 in Germany for friends and breeders of the White Miniature Schnauzers worldwide to promote interest and provide an informative network for sharing ideas and information and to give breeders the opportunity to exchange and expand their gene pool.

See also

- Standard Schnauzer
- Giant Schnauzer

Norfolk Terrier

The **Norfolk Terrier** is the smallest of the working Terriers. Prior to 1960, when it gained recognition as an independent breed, it was a variety of the Norwich Terrier, distinguished from the Norwich by its "drop", or folded ears.

Description

Appearance

The Norfolk Terrier has a wire-haired coat which, according to the various national kennel club breed standards, can be "all shadesh of red, wheaten, black and tan, or grizzle."

They are the smallest of the working Terriers. They are active and compact, free moving, with good substance and bone. Good substance means good spring of rib and bone that matches the body such that the dog can be a very agile ratter, the function for which it was bred.

Norfolk terriers are moderately proportioned dogs. A too heavy dog would not be agile. A too refined dog would make it a toy breed. Norfolks generally have more reach and drive and a stronger rear angulation, hence cover more ground than their Norwich cousins. Norfolk have good side gait owed to their balanced angulation front and rear and their slightly longer length of back.

The ideal height is 10 to 12 inches (25–30 cm) at the withers and weight is about 11 pounds (5 kg).

Temperament

Norfolks are described as fearless, but should not be aggressive despite being capable of defending themselves if need be. They, along with Norwich Terriers and Border Terriers, have the softest temperaments of the Terrier Group. Norfolks work in packs and must get along with other dogs. As companions, they love people and children and do make good pets. Their activity level is generally reflective of the pace of their environment. This breed should not be kept or live outside since they thrive on human contact. Generally, Norfolks are not given to digging but, like any dog, will dig out of boredom when left alone for too long a period. Norfolks can be barkers and are very vocal. They generally cohabit well with other household pets when introduced as a puppy. Outdoors, they are natural hunters with a strong prey drive for small vermin.

Norfolks are self confident and carry themselves with presence and importance, holding their heads and tails erect. A Norfolk that is shy or that carries its tail between its legs is atypical, as is a dog that is hot tempered and aggressive with other dogs; these traits are not the standard. A Norfolk's typical temperament is happy, spirited, and self confident. The greatest punishment to a dog is for his owner to ignore him.

Working style

Norfolks were originally bred as barn dogs to rid the barn of vermin. Some literature suggest that they were also occasionally used on the hunt to bolt animals of equal size from their den. To some extent they are still used in that capacity in continental Europe. Norfolks are pack animals and hence expected to get along with other dogs while working or in the home. As a pack dog, they take turns working their prey. They are fearless and their courage is incredible. Today, of course, they are household companions and must have an agreeable disposition for living with people.

Health

The life expectancy of a Norfolk Terrier is 12–15 years, with some growing as old as 19 years. Norfolks do have incidences of mitral valve disease, luxating patellas, and incorrect bites (where the teeth do not align with the breed standard, i.e. overshot or undershot). Norfolks most often have shallow hip sockets and many breedlines are dysplastic. There has never been a Norfolk Terrier recognized by the Orthopedic Foundation for Animals (OFA) as having "excellent" rated hips. Therefore responsible breeders are testing for hip dysplasia. Breeders that do not radiograph hips and have them evaluated by either OFA or PennHip, cannot answer questions regarding hip dysplasia in their breeding program.

Norfolks generally have small litters. Responsible breeders only breed healthy dogs who are of good temperament, good pedigree lineage and best reflect the breed standard. The demand for Norfolk is far greater than the supply. The environment in which they are raised directly impacts the temperament of the puppy for its lifetime.

Care

Grooming

These breeds have a double coat - a harsh, wiry topcoat and a soft, warm undercoat. Ideally, the coat is combed daily with a steel "greyhound " comb, but all that is really necessary for grooming a companion dog is a good combing once a week to remove the loose, dead hairs and prevent matting. As a minimum, the coat is hand stripped once in the Fall and once in the Spring. Clipping or cutting ruins the coat's colours and harsh texture. A Norfolk Terrier can be washed with a dog shampoo when dirty.

History

In the 1880s, British sportsmen developed a working terrier of East Anglia in Eastern England. The Norwich Terrier and later the drop-eared variety now know as the Norfolk Terrier, were believed to have been developed by crossing local terrier-like dogs, small, short-legged Irish Terrier breeds and the small red terriers used by the Gypsy ratters of Norfolk.

They were first called the **Cantab Terrier** when they became fashionable for students to keep in their rooms at Cambridge University in England. Later, they were called the **Trumpington Terrier**, after a street in the area where the breed was first developed. Then, just prior to World War I, an Irish horse rider named Frank Jones sold vast quantities of the short-legged terriers to the USA, so they were called the **Jones Terriers**.

In 1932, the Norwich was granted acceptance into the English Kennel Club and the first written standard was created. The American Kennel Club registered the first Norwich Terrier in 1936. In 1964, The Kennel Club reclassified the drop-ear variety as it its own breed, the Norfolk Terrier, and the prick-eared variety retained the name Norwich Terrier. The American Kennel Club and Canadian Kennel Club both recognized the division of the Norwich Terrier breed in 1979. The Norfolk Terrier was recognized by the United Kennel Club in 1979. After many generations, these two breeds have developed as two distinct breeds both in physical looks and in temperament. Of note, there is literature that suggests that the Norfolk and Norwich were always two distinct breeds and the original mistake was classifying them as one.

External links

- AKC The Norfolk and Norwich Terrier Club [1]
- The American Norfolk Terrier Association [2]
- The Norfolk Terrier Club of Great Britain [3]
- Norfolk Terrier club in Canada [4]
- Official Norfolk Terrier Club of Canada [5]

References

- The Norfolk Terrier [2], Third Edition, Joan R. Read, ANTA 2005 - available from the American Norfolk Terrier Association web site.
- Comparative Study & Illustrated Breed Standard of Norfolk and Norwich Terriers [6], Victor Sattler, Wildgoose Terriers (c) 2009 - out of print.

Norwich Terrier

The **Norwich Terrier** is a breed of dog. It originates in the United Kingdom and was bred to hunt small vermin or rodents.

Description

Appearance

These terriers are one of the smallest terriers (11-12 lb, 5-5.4 kg; 9-10 inches (24-25.5 cm) at the withers), with prick ears and a double coat, which come in red, tan, wheaten, black and tan, and grizzle.

Temperament

These small but hardy dogs are courageous, remarkably intelligent and wonderfully affectionate. They can be assertive but it is not typical for them to be aggressive, quarrelsome or shy. They are energetic and thrive on an active life. They are eager to please but have definite minds of their own. They are sensitive to scolding but 100% Terrier. They should never be kept outside or in a kennel setting because they love the companionship of their owners too much. Norwich are not given to unnecessary barking but they will warn of a stranger approaching. Norwich are good with children. If introduced to other household pets as a puppy they generally co-habit peacefully, though caution should be observed around rodent pets as they may be mistaken for prey.

Health

The life expectancy of the Norwich Terrier is 12–16 years. While the Norwich Terrier is considered a healthy breed, there are some health issues for which responsible breeders do preventative genetic health testing, thereby reducing the incidences.

The Norwich Terrier does have a predilection for some health issues but studies to determine the exact mode of inheritance or the exact frequency in the breed are unknown or have not been conclusive. At present there are no disorders identified as "most important". Of secondary magnitude, cataracts are recognized as a disorder that has been reported sporadically and may be inherited. Also of a secondary magnitude there are instances of epilepsy, narrow tracheas, luxating patellas, hip dysplasia, mitral valve disease, [atopylatopy(allergic inhalant dermatitis)] and incorrect bites (how the teeth meet when the jaws are closed).

Like all dogs, Norwich Terriers can have autoimmune reactivity to rabies vaccinations. Rabies-Vaccine-Induced Ischemic Dermatopathy, or RVI-ID, is a non-fatal but potentially serious reaction to chemicals called adjuvants in the vaccine. RVI-ID is often misdiagnosed, but if correctly diagnosed, is treatable. Symptoms may include: symmetrical dark spots or lesions at the tips of the ears; swelling, hard lumps or dark spots in the vicinity of the injection site.

Higher volume Norwich breeders are seeing more dogs with breathing concerns, and the Norwich and Norfolk Terrier Club (USA) has formed a new "Health and Genetics Sub-Committee for Research on Upper Airway Syndrome in Norwich Terriers". Upper Airway Syndrome (UAS) covers all abnormalities that can occur in the upper airway, including: elongated soft palates; too short soft palates; narrow/misshapen tracheas; collapsing tracheas; stenotic nares (nasal passages that are too small); swollen tonsils; everted laryngeal saccules. These upper airway disorders can occur singly or in combination with one or two others. All compromise the airway and the dog's ability to breathe normally; the dog's breathing often sounds raspy or moist. It may be that shorter muzzles may have increased incidence of such issues.

Norwich Terriers generally have small litters of 1 to 3 puppies. Generally, if a female is healthy, its optimal breeding period is between the ages of 2 (after all genetic health testing is complete - heart, eyes, hips and petellas) and six years. At seven years of age dogs are considered geriatric. The small supply and the high price of a pure bred Norwich Terrier - often around US$2,500 in 2008 - has attracted fraud, as unsuspecting buyers pay full price for Cairn Terriers with docked tails, or mixed-breed puppies.

In the Canada and the United States you can verify if a dog has completed genetic health testing by checking the open registry at www.offa.org.

Care

Exercise requirements

Norwich Terriers are hardy, active dogs, bred for a working life of pursuing vermin and accompanying their farmer owners on horseback. A good daily walk is therefore the minimum needed to meet the exercise requirements of a healthy Norwich Terrier. Norwich Terriers compete in Earthdog competitions, and are increasingly common in Agility and Flyball competitions. The dogs were bred as working terriers, and thrive best with at least one hour of real activity daily, such as a good walk, run, or working session. Norwich are curious, independent dogs who may become bored by routine, repetitive walks/routes.

Grooming

The Norwich Terrier has two coats - a harsh, wiry topcoat and a soft warm undercoat. Ideally, the coat is combed with a steel comb daily to once a week to remove the loose, dead hairs and prevent matting. Proper maintenance of the Norwich coat, like other hard wiry coats, requires "stripping," or pulling the oldest hairs from the coat (using fingers and/or a "stripping knife," a special grooming comb). Stripping results both in the coat retaining its proper appearance, and in the health of the dog's skin and coat. Ideally, owners hand-strip the coat on a regular basis to achieve what is called a "rolling" coat, where hairs of all lengths are growing in. Maintaining a rolling coat is easier on the dog's skin and requires shorter grooming sessions. At minimum, the coat should be stripped once in the autumn and once in the spring. Clipping or cutting negatively affects the appearance of the coat's natural colours and texture. For a very helpful article on how to groom the Norwich Terrier's coat see Wildgoose's Grooming Norwich Terriers and Norfolk Terriers [1].

Tail docking

Outside of Canada and the United States, the docked-tail profile of the Norwich Terrier is changing. In Australia tail docking is optional.But in NSW it is illegal. In the United Kingdom tail docking is only permitted for working dogs and is banned for dogs bred as pets or showing. Some countries banned general tail docking for a number of years e.g. Norway since 1987, Sweden since 1988. In the last four years Cyprus, Greece, Luxembourg and Switzerland have decided to introduce a ban on tail docking. In the United States, a docked tail is currently considered "strongly preferred" for success in the show ring.

Proponents of docking argue that a docked-tail dog can be extracted from a hole by the tail with less risk to the dog's spine. Opponents of tail docking note that docking severely damages the important canine tail-signalling system, so vital to dogs' social encounters, and also cite the historical basis of docking in the UK to avoid taxation of sporting dogs.

Breeding

Norwich Terriers are difficult to breed. Many have Caesarean sections. The North American average litter size for 2007 is two puppies with the total number of puppies for the year, in the USA, at approximately 750. There are breeding lines with higher average litter sizes as can be easily traced in pedigrees of kennel clubs who include such information, i.e. The Dutch Kennel Club. Similar information can be obtained at internet site of Finnish Kennel Club.

Recently in the United States, there has been significant pedigree fraud . Sometimes these fake Norwich Terriers are sold over the internet.

History

The breed has existed since at least the late 1800s, as working terrier of East Anglia, England. The dogs were useful as ratters in the stable yard, bolters of fox for the hunt, and family companions. It was the mascot of students at Cambridge University. Small red terriers, descendants of Irish Terriers, had existed in the area since at least the 1860s, and these might be the ancestors of the Norwich, or it might have come from the Trumpington Terrier, a breed that no longer exists. In its earliest history, it was also known as the *Jones Terrier* and the *Cantab Terrier*.

Since its earliest identification as a breed, puppies have had either drop or prick ears, and both were allowed when the Norwich was first recognized in the show ring in 1932 by The Kennel Club (England). Drop ears were often cropped until it became illegal to do so. This intensified a long-standing controversy over whether drop-eared dogs should be allowed in the show ring and whether the primary difference was simply the ears or whether other, deeper, personality and structural differences marked the drop-eared variety. Starting in the 1930s, breeders increased their efforts to distinguish the breeds. While Norfolk and Norwich Terriers were inter-bred for a number of years today they are positively two distinctive breeds. In fact some historical texts indicate that they were distinctive breeds before they were inter-bred.

Both ear types continued to be allowed in the ring until The Kennel Club recognized the drop-eared variety as a separate breed, the Norfolk Terrier, in 1964, and the American Kennel Club, United Kennel Club, and Canadian Kennel Club did the same in 1979. Until that time the breeds were designated by the AKC as Norwich Terriers, P.E. (prick ears) and Norwich Terriers, D.E. (drop ears).

External links

- UK based Norwich Terrier Forum [2]
- Norwich Terrier Club of America [3]

Parson Russell Terrier

The **Parson Russell terrier** was recognized by the UK Kennel Club in 1990, followed by Australia and FCI countries, then American Kennel Club in 2001, as Parson Jack Russell terrier and then in the United States as the Parson Russell terrier. Because the name "Jack Russell terrier" was trade-marked in the USA by a group of people who did not wish to become a part of an all-breed kennel club, the American Kennel Club made a compromise with the Jack Russell Terrier Club of America to change the breeds name to "Parson Russell" terrier. The rest of the world now recognizes the Jack Russell and the Parson Russell as 2 separate breeds.

The Parson Russell Terrier is descended from early primarily white-bodied foxing terriers used in the hunt field. At the end of the 19th Century, these dogs were drawn into the Kennel Club as "fox terriers," but their still-working antecedents were referred to as "Jack Russell" terriers throughout the 20th Century in honor of the Rev. John "Jack" Russell, a noted fox hunter of the 19th Century "The Sporting Parson" who is credited with creating the breed.

Breed Standard

The ideal height of a mature dog is 14" at the highest point of the shoulder blade, and bitches 13". The weight of a terrier in hard working condition is usually between 13-17 lb. The terrier should appear balanced and proportionate with the height at withers is slightly greater than the distance from the withers to tail. These terries have medium bone, which is not so heavy as to appear coarse or so light as to appear racy. The head is to be proportionate with the body with small V-shaped drop ears and a full pigmented black nose. The bite should be a scissor bite with the top set of teeth very slightly overlapping the bottom. The coat can be smooth or broken, consisting of a double coat which is naturally harsh, close and dense, straight with no suggestion of kink. There is a clear outline with only a hint of eyebrows and beard if natural to the coat. This terrier is intended to be shown in his natural appearance and not excessively groomed. Their color is predominantly white with black or tan markings, or a combination of these. Colors are clear but grizzle is acceptable and should not be confused with brindle (which would disqualify the terrier).

Temperament

The Parson is a bold and energetic happy go lucky terrier. They often do well with people who possess those same attributes as well as patience and a sense of humor. Parsons can do very well with children, but many Parsons won't tolerate being handled roughly, so it is not recommended that they be placed in homes with very young children. Parsons do not do well in flats or apartments because of their high exercise requirements. Because the Parson was bred to hunt, it can be difficult for them to live with some pets such as small rodents. While they will get along fine with cats if raised with them, it is not recommended to leave them together unsupervised. They are very intelligent and eager to please. Many excel in activities such as obedience, agility, conformation and earthdog.

Grooming

The grooming requirements for the Parson Russell terrier can vary depending on whether it has a broken coat or a smooth coat. For the broken coat brushing is required once weekly, and its coat may need to be hand stripped every few months. The smooth coated variety is lower in maintenance, and its coat simply needs to be "brushed" occasionally with a groomers stone to keep it looking good. These dogs are medium shedders, and do shed all year round, with the smooth coats sheding the most.

Origin

This terrier finds its origins in 19th century England by a clergyman named Jack Russell. This feisty little terrier was used to hunt small game, particularly fox, by digging to the quarry and either holding it or bolting it from its den.

See also

- Jack Russell terrier
- Russell terrier

Resources

- http://www.akc.org/breeds/parson_russell_terrier/
- http://www.dogbreedinfo.com/parsonrussellterrier.htm
- http://www.justdogbreeds.com/parson-russell-terrier.html
- http://www.redrockparsons.com/parson-russell-history.html

External links

- Parson Russell Terrier Association of America [1]
- A Pictorial History of Terriers [2]
- Parson Russell Terrier Club (UK) [3]

Scottish Terrier

Scottie redirects here; distinguish from Scotty.

The **Scottish Terrier** (also known as the **Aberdeen Terrier**), popularly called the **Scottie**, is a breed of dog. Initially one of the highland breeds of Terrier that were grouped under the name of *Skye Terrier*, it is one of five breeds of terrier that originated in Scotland, the other four being the modern Skye, Cairn, Dandie Dinmont, and West Highland White Terrier. They are an independent and rugged breed with a wiry outer coat and a soft dense undercoat. The Fourth Earl of Dumbarton nicknamed the breed "the diehard." The modern breed is said to be able to trace its lineage back to a single female, named Splinter II.

They are a small breed of Terrier with a distinctive shape and have had many roles in popular culture. They have been owned by a variety of celebrities, including the 43rd President of the United States George W. Bush, and are well known for being a playing piece in the board game Monopoly. Described as a territorial, feisty dog, they can make a good watchdog and tend to be very loyal to their family. In health issues, Scottish Terriers can be more prone to bleeding disorders, joint disorders, autoimmune diseases, allergies, and cancer than some other breeds of dog and there is a condition named after the breed called Scotty cramp. They are also one of the more successful dog breeds at the Westminster Kennel Club Dog Show with a recent best in show in 2010.

Description

Appearance

A Scottish Terrier is a small but resilient terrier with a muscular body and neck (a typical neck circumference is 14 inches), often appearing to be barrel chested. They are short-legged, cobby and sturdily built, with a long head in proportion to their size. The Scottie should have large paws adapted for digging. Erect ears and tail are salient features of the breed. Their eyes are small, bright and almond-shaped and dark brown or nearly black in colour.

Height at withers for both genders should be roughly , and the length of back from withers to tail is roughly . Generally a well-balanced Scottie dog should weigh from and a female from . It is about in height.

The Scottie typically has a hard, wiry, long, weather-resistant outer coat and a soft dense under coat. The coat is typically trimmed and blended, with a longer coat on the beard, eyebrows, legs and lower body — traditionally shaggy-to-the-ground. The head, ears, tail and back are traditionally trimmed short.

The coat colors range from dark gray to jet black, or 'Brindle' (a mix of black and brown). Scotties with 'Wheaten' (straw to nearly white) coats sometimes occur, but should not be confused with the

Soft-Coated Wheaten Terrier or West Highland White Terrier.

Temperament

Scotties are territorial, alert, quick moving and feisty, perhaps even more so than other terrier breeds. The breed is known to be independent and self-assured, playful, intelligent and has been nicknamed the 'Diehard' because of its rugged nature and endless determination. The 'Diehard' nickname was originally given to it in the 19th century by George, the fourth Earl of Dumbarton. The Earl had a famous pack of Scottish Terriers, so brave that they were named "Diehards". They were supposed to have inspired the name of his Regiment, The Royal Scots, "Dumbarton's Diehards".

Scotties, while being described as very loving, have also been described as stubborn. They are sometimes described as an aloof breed, although it has been noted that they tend to be very loyal to their family and are known to attach themselves to one or two people.

It has been suggested that the Scottish Terrier can make a good watchdog due to its tendency to bark only when necessary and because it is typically reserved with strangers, although this is not always the case. They have been described as a fearless breed that may be aggressive around other dogs unless introduced at an early age. Scottish Terriers were originally bred to hunt and fight badgers. Therefore, the Scottie is prone to dig as well as chase small vermin, such as Squirrels, rats, and mice.

Health

Two genetic health concerns seen in the breed are von Willebrand disease (vWD) and craniomandibular osteopathy (CMO); Scottie cramp, patellar luxation and cerebellar abiotrophy are also sometimes seen in this breed. Common eye conditions seen in a variety of breeds such as cataracts and glaucoma can appear in Scotties as they age. There are no specific conditions relating the skin that affect the breed, but they can be affected by common dog related conditions such as parasites and mange. Scotties typically live from 11 and 13 years.

Cancer in Scottish Terriers

Scottish Terriers have a greater chance of developing some cancers than other purebreds. According to research by the Veterinary Medical Data Program (1986), six cancers that Scotties appeared to be more at risk for (when compared to other breeds) are: (in descending order) bladder cancer and other transitional cell carcinomas of the lower urinary tract; malignant melanoma; gastric carcinoma; squamous cell carcinoma of the skin; lymphosarcoma and nasal carcinoma. Other cancers that are known to commonly affect Scotties include mast cell sarcoma and hemangiosarcoma.

Research has suggested that Scottish Terriers are 20 times more likely to get bladder cancer than other breeds and the most common kind of bladder cancer is transitional cell carcinoma of the bladder (TCC). Dr. Deborah Knapp of Purdue University School of Veterinary Medicine has commented "TCC usually occurs in older dogs (average age 11 years) and is more common in females (2:1 ratio of females to males)." Symptoms of TCC are blood in the urine, straining to urinate, and frequent urination — although owners noticing any of these symptoms should also be aware that the same symptoms may also be indicative of a urinary tract infection.

The most common and effective form of treatment for TCC is Piroxicam, a non-steroidal anti-inflammatory drug that "allows the cancer cells to kill themselves." In order to help prevent cancer in a dog, an owner should ensure that their dog has minimal exposure to herbicides, pesticides, solvents and cigarette smoke; use caution when treating dogs with some flea medications; provide a healthy, vitamin-rich diet (low in carbohydrates, high in vegetables) and plenty of exercise.

Scottie cramp

Scottie cramp is an autosomal recessive hereditary disorder which inhibits the dog's ability to walk. It is caused by a defect in the pathways in the brain that control muscle contraction due to a low level of serotonin in the body. Typically symptoms only show when the particular dog is under some degree of stress. The front legs are pushed out to the side, the back arches and the rear legs overflex, causing the dog to fall should they be moving at speed. The condition is not seizure related, and the dog remains conscious throughout the event, with symptoms abating once the cause of the stress has been removed.

It does not worsen with age, and Vitamin E, Diazepam and Prozac have all been shown to be effective treatments should it be required. Serotonin inhibitors such as aspirin or penicillin have been found to make the condition worsen. Scotty cramp is found in other breeds of Terrier, including the Cesky Terrier. "Episodic Falling", a condition found in Cavalier King Charles Spaniels is considered to be similar to this disorder.

Craniomandibular osteopathy

Also known as "Lion Jaw", "Westy Jaw" or "Scotty Jaw", this condition of craniomandibular osteopathy is caused by excessive bone growth in the bottom jaw, usually occurring between four to seven months of age. Like Scottie Cramp, it is a autosomal recessive hereditary disorder, and can cause discomfort to the dog when it attempts to chew. The progression of the condition usually slows down between eleven to thirteen months of age, and is sometimes followed by a slow partial or complete regression.

This condition has also been seen in other breeds of dog, such as the West Highland White Terrier, Cairn Terrier, Boston Terrier, as well as some larger breeds such as Bullmastiffs.

von Willebrand's disease

Von Willebrand's disease is a hereditary bleeding disorder found in both dogs and humans. It is caused by a lack of von Willebrand factor which plays a role in the clotting process of blood. This can cause abnormal platelet function and prolonged bleeding times. Affected dogs can be prone to nose bleeds, and increased bleeding following trauma or surgery. There are three types of this condition with Type I being the most common, while Type II and III being rarer, but more severe. Type I von Willebrand's disease is relatively common in the Scottish Terrier.

Type I is more widespread in Doberman Pinscher, but is as common in the Shetland Sheepdog as the Scottish Terrier. The condition appears in most breeds to some extent, but other breeds with an increased risk include the Golden Retriever, German Shepherd Dog, Basset Hound and Manchester Terrier.

History

Initial grouping of several of the highland terriers (including the Scottie) under the generic name *Skye terriers* caused some confusion in the breed's lineage. There is disagreement over whether the Skye terriers mentioned in early 16th century records actually descended from forerunners of the Scottie or vice versa. It is certain, however, that Scotties and West Highland White Terriers are closely related — both their forefathers originated from the Blackmount region of Perthshire and the Moor of Rannoch. Scotties were originally bred to hunt and kill vermin on farms and to hunt badgers and foxes in the Highlands of Scotland.

The actual origin of a breed as old as the Scottish Terrier is obscure and undocumented. The first written records about a dog of similar description to the Scottish Terrier dates from 1436, when Don Leslie described them in his book *The History of Scotland 1436-1561*. Two hundred years later, Sir Joshua Reynolds painted a portrait of a young girl caressing a dog similar in appearance to the modern-day Scottie. King James VI of Scotland was an important historical figure featuring in the Scottish Terrier's history. In the 17th century, when King James VI became James I of England, he sent six terriers — thought to be forerunners of the Scottish terrier — to a French monarch as a gift. His love and adoration for the breed increased their popularity throughout the world.

Many dog writers after the early 1800s seem to agree that there were two varieties of terrier existing in Britain at the time — a rough-haired so-called Scotch Terrier and a smooth-haired English Terrier. Thomas Brown, in his *Biological Sketches and Authentic Anecdotes of Dogs* (1829), states that "the Scotch terrier is certainly the purest in point of breed and the (smooth) English seems to have been produced by a cross from him". Brown went on to describe the Scotch Terrier as "low in stature, with a strong muscular body, short stout legs, a head large in proportion to the body" and was "generally of a sandy colour or black" with a "long, matted and hard" coat. Although the Scotch Terrier described here is more generic than specific to a breed, it asserts the existence of a small, hard, rough-coated terrier developed for hunting small game in the Scottish Highlands in the early 1800s; a description that shares characteristics with what was once known as the Aberdeen Terrier and is today known as the Scottish Terrier. In addition, the paintings of Sir Edwin Landseer and an 1835 lithograph entitled "Scottish Terriers at Work on a Cairn in the West Highlands" both depict Scottie type terriers very similar to those described in the first Scottish Terrier Standard.

In the 1800s, the Highlands of Scotland, including the Isle of Skye, were abundant with terriers originally known by the generic term "short-haired" or "little Skye terriers." Towards the end of the 19th century, it was decided to separate these Scottish terriers and develop pure bloodlines and specific breeds. Originally, the breeds were separated into two categories — Dandie Dinmont Terriers and Skye Terriers (not the Skye Terrier known today, but a generic name for a large group of terriers with differing traits all said to originate from the Isle of Skye). The Birmingham England dog show of 1860 was the first to offer classes for these groups of terriers. They continued to be exhibited in generic groups for several years and these groups included the ancestors of today's Scottish Terrier. Recorded history and the initial development of the breed started in the late 1870s with the development of dog shows. The exhibition and judging of dogs required comparison to a breed standard and thus the appearance and temperament of the Scottie was written down for the first time. Eventually, the Skye Terriers were further divided into what are known today as the Scottish Terrier, Skye Terrier, West Highland White Terrier and Cairn Terrier.

While fanciers sought to identify and standardize the breed and its description through the late 1800s, the Scottish terrier was known by many different names: the Highland, the Cairn, Diehard, and most often, the Aberdeen Terrier — named because of the abundant number of the dogs in the area and because a J.A. Adamson of Aberdeen successfully exhibited his dogs during the 1870s. Roger Rough, a dog owned by Adamson, Tartan, a dog owned by Mr Paynton Piggott, Bon Accord, a dog owned by Messrs. Ludlow and Bromfield and Splinter II, owned by Mr Ludlow, were early winners of dog exhibitions and are the four dogs from which all Scottish Terrier pedigrees ultimately begin. It is often said that all present day Scotties stem from a single bitch, Splinter II, and two sires. In her book, *The New Scottish Terrier*, Cindy Cooke refers to Splinter II as the "foundation matron of the modern Scottish Terrier." Cooke goes on to say "For whatever reason, early breeders line bred on this bitch to the virtual exclusion of all others. Mated to Tartan, she produced Worry, the dam of four champions. Rambler, her son by Bonaccord, sired the two founding sires of the breed, *Ch. Dundee* (out of Worry) and *Ch. Alistair* (out of a Dundee daughter)" Show champions on both sides of the Atlantic descend from Splinter and her sires.

Captain Gordon Murray and S.E. Shirley were responsible for setting the type in 1879. Shortly afterwards, in 1879, Scotties were for the first time exhibited at Alexander Palace in England, while the following year they began to be classified in much the same way as is done today. The first written standard of the breed was drafted by J.B. Morrison and D.J. Thomson Gray and appeared in Vero Shaw's *Illustrated Book of The Dog*, published in 1880; it was extremely influential in setting both breed type and name. The standard described the breed's colouring as "Grey, Grizzle or Brindle", as the typically Black colouring of Scotties did not become fashionable or favoured until the 1900s.

In 1881 the "Scottish Terrier Club of England" was founded, being the first club dedicated to the breed. The club secretary, H.J. Ludlow, is responsible for greatly popularising the breed in the southern parts of Great Britain. The "Scottish Terrier Club of Scotland" was not founded until 1888, seven years after the English club. Following the formation of the English and Scottish clubs there followed several years of disagreement regarding the breed's official standard. The issue was finally settled by a revised standard in 1930, which was based on four prepotent dogs. The dogs were Robert and James Chapman's Heather Necessity, Albourne Barty, bred by AG Cowley, Albourne Annie Laurie, bred by Miss Wijk and Miss Wijk's Marksman of Docken (the litter brother of Annie Laurie). These four dogs and their offspring modified the look of the Scottie, particularly the length of the head, closeness to the ground and the squareness of body. Their subsequent success in the show ring led to them becoming highly sought after by the British public and breeders. As such, the modified standard completely revolutionized the breed. This new standard was subsequently recognised by the Kennel Club UK circa 1930.

Scotties were introduced to America in the early 1890s but it was not until the years between World War I and World War II that the breed became popular. A club was formed in 1900 and a standard written in 1925. The Scottish Terrier was recognized by the United Kennel Club in 1934. By 1936, Scotties were the third most popular breed in the United States. Although they did not permanently stay in fashion, they continue to enjoy a steady popularity with a large segment of the dog-owning public across the world.

Scottish Terriers have won best in show at the Westminster Kennel Club Dog Show more than any other breed except for the Wire Fox Terrier, a total of nine times. These victories began in 1911 with a win by Ch. Tickle Em Jock and include recent victories such as in 1995 when Ch. Gaelforce Post Script won, and in 2010 with a victory by Ch. Roundtown Mercedes Of Maryscot.

Famous Scotties and popular culture

The Scottie is the only breed of dog that has lived in the White House more than three times. President Franklin D. Roosevelt was renowned for owning a Scottie named Fala, a gift from his cousin, Margaret Stuckley. The President loved Fala so much that he rarely went anywhere without him. Roosevelt had several Scotties before Fala, including one named Duffy and another named Mr. Duffy. Eleanor Roosevelt had a Scottish Terrier named Meggie when the family entered the White House in 1933. More recently, President George W. Bush has owned two black Scottish terriers, Barney and Miss Beazley. Barney starred in nine films produced by the White House, including Barney Cam VII: A Red, White and Blue Christmas. Other famous people who are known to have owned Scotties include: Queen Victoria, Eva Braun, Dwight D. Eisenhower, Jacqueline Kennedy Onassis, Ed Whitfield and President of Poland, Lech Kaczynski. Actress Tatum O'Neal owned a Scottish Terrier. She was said to be so saddened by her dog's death to cancer and old age that she relapsed into drugs.

The Scottie is also renowned for being featured in the popular board game, Monopoly, as a player token. When the game was first created in the 1930s, Scotties were one of the most popular pets in the United States, and it is also one of the most popular Monopoly game tokens, according to Matt Collins, vice president of marketing for Hasbro.

A Scottish Terrier and a West Highland White Terrier are featured on the Black & White whisky label, and the breed has been used as the mascot for the Chum brand of dog food, appearing on both the brand's packaging and TV commercials. Scottish Terriers are also part of the emblem for the clothing line Juicy Couture and Radley handbags.

In May 2007, Carnegie Mellon University named the Scottish Terrier its official mascot. The Scottie had been a long-running unofficial mascot of the university, whose founder's Scottish heritage is also honored by the official athletic nickname of "Tartans." During the opening of the May, 2007, Carnegie Mellon commencement ceremony, keynote speaker Bill Cosby, a Scottie fancier, led the university's new mascot, named Scottie, to the speaker's platform. Agnes Scott College in Decatur, Georgia also uses the Scottie as their mascot.

See also

- List of domesticated Scottish breeds
- Scotty dog sign (radiological term)

Mixes

- Bushland Terrier Scottish Terrier/Cairn Terrier

Sealyham Terrier

The **Sealyham Terrier** is a dog breed, of the terrier type. The Sealyham Terrier was originally developed in Wales.

Appearance

Sealyhams measurements vary by breed standard according to particular countries. In general, the breed should measure between 10 1/2 up to 12 inches in height, measured at the wither, or top of the shoulder blade. Sealyhams should never exceed 12 inches at the withers. They should weigh between 23-25 pounds, males being heavier. Length of back should approximate the height. Length of back is measured from the top of the withers to the front edge of the tail. Coat color is always white and marking colours include lemon, brown, and badger; which is a mix of brown and black. Black markings are not preferred since they appear harsh in contrast to the white coat. While black markings appear in the breed, black markings are not allowed in any breed standard in any country. Black markings are sometimes referred to as blue markings, which are also not allowed in any country's breed standard. Ticking (speckled markings) on the body are acceptable. Sealyhams may have body markings; speckled ticking and larger body color markings, all of which are acceptable.

Temperament

A Sealyham puppy is normally very active. As the Sealyham matures, it becomes a couch potato, "displaying an even temper and a calm and relaxed attitude". Sealyhams are not busy dogs so it is necessary to manage their weight through calorie management and occasional exercise, such as a daily walk.

Grooming

Sealyham coats are groomed by stripping, in order to keep the coat from becoming too soft.

History

The Sealyham Terrier derives its name from Sealyham, Haverfordwest, Wales, the estate of Captain John Edwardes, who developed a strain of dogs noted for their prowess in quarrying small game. He crossed the Dandie Dinmont, the now-extinct White English Terrier, the Fox Terrier, the West Highland White Terrier, and the Corgie, and tested the offspring for hunting ability, culling those who did not prove game.

Within the Hollywood Movie Industry, the Sealyham became a fashionable dog to own by the Hollywood elite. It was owned by Director Alfred Hitchcock, Actors, Jean Harlow, Cary Grant,

Elizabeth Taylor, Princess Margaret. The dog was widely owned in England, but interest in the dog waned in conjunction with the banning of badger digs. Today it is primarily a companion dog, and when hunting has been banned in countries, its use for hunting purposes has been eliminated.

The first Sealyham Terrier club was created in 1908 and the breed was officially recognised in 1910. The Sealyham Terrier now is recognised by all of the major kennel clubs in the English-speaking world. The Sealyham was once one of the more popular terriers and one of the best known Welsh breeds. Today, however, The Kennel Club (UK) lists the Sealyham as amongst the most endangered native breeds..

A Sealyham Terrier, Champion Efbe's Hidalgo At Goodspice, won Best In Show at Crufts in 2009.

Famous Sealyham Terriers

- Efbe's Hidalgo At Goodspice (Charmin) became *World Champion* (Best in Show) at the Fédération Cynologique Internationale 2008 Stockholm, Sweden World Dog Show. Charmin also won the 2007 AKC/Eukanuba National Championship Best of Show and 2009 Best in Show at Crufts. Charmin has featured in Eukanuba advertisements.
- Jennie, pet of Maurice Sendak, featured in his book *Higglety, Pigglety, Pop!* (Sendak included Sealyhams in many of his other works as well, most notably *Where the Wild Things Are*).
- At the beginning of the Alfred Hitchcock film *The Birds*, Hitchcock (in his cameo appearance for the film) is walking his two Sealyham Terriers - Geoffrey and Stanley - out of a shop as Tippi Hedren walks in. Hitchcock also owned a third Sealyham named Mr. Jenkins.
- At the end of the movie The Departed when Matt Damon exits the elevator, a Sealyham Terrier makes a short appearance as it is walked by an old lady to the same elevator.

See also

- Welsh Terrier
- Welsh Corgi

Skye Terrier

The **Skye Terrier** is a breed of dog that is a long, low terrier and hardy.

Appearance

Coat

The Skye is double coated, with a short, soft undercoat and a hard, straight topcoat. The ideal coat length is 5 1/2 inches (14 cm), with no extra credit for a longer coat. The shorter hair of the head veils the forehead and eyes, forming a moderate beard. The ears should be well feathered and, in prick-eared examples, the hair should fall like a fringe, accenting the form, and blending with the side locks.

Colour

Fawn, blue, dark or light grey, blonde, and black with black points (ears and muzzle) all occur. They may have any self colour, allowing for some shading of same colour on the body and a lighter undercoat, so long as the nose and ears are black. There should be no further patterning on the body, but a small white spot on the chest is permissible.

Types

Except for the shape and size of the ears, there is no significant difference nor preference given between the prick- and drop-eared types. When prick, they are medium sized, carried high on the skull and angled slightly outwards. In the drop type, the ears are set lower, are larger, and should hang flat against the head, with little or no muscle movement forwards and backwards.

Grooming

The Skye Terrier coat is resistant to tangling, and needs to be brushed at least once a week. The Skye should be generally kept natural and untrimmed; however, minor trimming of the coat between and around the toes and pads can help avoid problems due to trapped dampness or twigs, pebbles, mud, etc.

Health

Being an achondroplastic dog breed with extremely short legs, the Skye Terrier has particular health concerns. The most preventable is often called *Skye limp* or *Puppy limp*, and it is due to premature closure of the distal radial growth plate. If a Skye is exercised too often, too young, especially before 8 months, they can damage their bone growth, leading to a painful limp and possibly badly bowed legs. Jumping up and down from objects, climbing over objects, running, even long walks, are all things to be avoided for the first 8 to 10 months to prevent later problems and allow for correct closure of the growth plate.

Degenerative disc disease is also a common problem in short-legged dogs, and as many as 10% of Skyes will suffer from it.

Mammary cancer is the leading cause of Skye Terrier deaths, with Hemangiosarcomas (a malignant tumour of the blood vessels), Autoimmune disease, and Hyperthyroidism[1] as other concerns of the breed.

Overall, the breed is still considered quite healthy, and the average lifespan is 12-15 years.

Under threat

There are concerns that the breed is under threat of extinction with only 30 born in the UK in 2005[2]. It is today the most endangered of the Vulnerable Native Breeds of this country, and within 40 years the breed may disappear completely.[3].

History

There are at least two versions of the history of the Skye terrier. It was before accepted that the Skye Terrier's origins are connected with a centuries old shipwreck. The story goes that early in the 1600's a Spanish ship wrecked on the Isle of Skye in the Scottish Hebrides. Some of the survivors of the shipwreck were Maltese dogs that mated with the local terriers, creating a new and unique breed of Terrier. But a text of Caius, written decades before the shipwreck, describes a very modern portrait of the Skye terrier, proving that the modern Skye terrier existed long time before the arrival of the Malteses :

> "lap dogs which were brought out of the barbarous borders from the uttermost countryes northward, and they by reason of the length of their heare, make show neither face nor body, and yet these curres forsooth because they are so strange, are greatly set by, esteemed, taken up, and made of, in room of the spaniell gentle, or comforter".

So it is sure that the Skye terrier has inherited very few, or even not, characteristics of the Maltese. As an achondroplastic breed, and looking alike the Welsh corgi, it is believed that the Skye Terrier may have been a result of a crossing between the celtic terriers local to the area and the Swedish Vallhund of the Viking invaders. It may be that the Swedish Vallhund had mated with the local terriers centuries before Maltese dogs were said to have arrived, making both histories true.

The Skye Terrier was recognized by the United Kennel Club on January 1, 1993.

See also

- List of domesticated Scottish breeds

External links

- Skye Terrier Club of America [4]
- Skye Canada [5]
- Skye Terrier Club (UK) [6]
- The Skye Terrier Foundation [7]
- The Skye Terrier World Web Directory [8]

Fox Terrier (Smooth)

The **Smooth Fox Terrier** is a breed of dog, one of many terrier breeds. It was the first breed in the fox terrier family to be given official recognition by The Kennel Club (circa 1875; breed standard 1876). It is well known, and although not a widely popular breed today outside of hunting and show circles, it is extremely significant due to the large number of terriers believed descended from it.

Description

Appearance

The Smooth Fox Terrier is a balanced, well-proportioned terrier with a distinctive head that has a tapering muzzle, fiery dark eyes, and folded v-shaped ears set well up on the head, but not prick. It is a sturdy dog in that it is well-muscled and exhibits endurance, but should not appear in any way coarse or cloddy.

The male Fox terrier is tame but it will also respond to your commands. Shoulder height of a male Smooth Fox Terrier should be no taller than 15.5" with females proportionally less, and a male in show condition should weigh approximately 18 lbs.

The tail should be set well up on the back and be straight or slightly curved, but not carried over the back or curled like an Akita's.

Its coat is hard, flat, and abundant. This breed does shed somewhat. In color they should be predominantly white—some are even all white—but typically have markings of black and tan. Red, liver, or brindle are objectionable and disqualifying faults in the show ring. Heads are usually solid colored, but a variety of white markings are permissible, including half or split faces, blazes, or color only over the eyes and/or ears. It is commonly tri-colored.

Temperament

Smooth Fox Terriers make excellent family pets. Because this is an intelligent and active breed, they must be kept exercised, and interested, and a part of the family. They are affectionate and playful. They have well-developed hunting instincts. Left to their own devices and deprived of human companionship, undesirable behaviour may be exhibited, including chasing of small animals, or escaping if ignored.

History

The Smooth Fox Terrier's development as a breed is largely undocumented, but the dog has been known as a distinct breed in England since at least the 18th century; the first documented evidence of the Smooth Fox Terrier came in 1790, when a man by the name of Colonel Thornton painted a portrait of his beloved dog, Pitch.

The Smooth Fox Terrier entered the show ring during the mid-1800s, making it one of the earliest entrants in such events. The American Kennel Club recognized the Fox Terrier in 1885; one hundred years later, the Smooth Fox Terrier was recognized as being a distinct breed from the Wire Fox Terrier.

Conventional wisdom long held that the Smooth Fox Terrier and Wire Fox Terrier are variations of the same breed; in recent years, however, an increasing number of experts have stated the opinion that the two breeds are not related at all. Whereas the Wire Fox Terrier is probably directly descended from the Rough Black and Tan Terrier of Wales, the Smooth Fox Terrier is thought to count the Smooth Black and Tan as its primary ancestor, with traces of Beagle and Bull Terrier thrown in as well.

However, the two breeds were considered to be varieties of one breed and were occasionally interbred until the mid-1980s when the AKC changed them from varieties to separate breeds. All modern Smooth Fox Terriers trace back to wires many times, from Eng. Ch Watteau Chorister, through Eng. Ch. Lethal Weapon, Eng. Ch. Corrector of Notts and Eng. Ch. Cromwell Ochre's Legacy back to Dusky D'Orsay. Bred by Mr. Francis Redmond, Dusky D'Orsay's sire was a Wire, Dusky Collar, and her dam a Smooth, Eng. Ch. D'Orsay's Donna. Through Dusky D'Orsay, all modern Smooths trace back to several famous Wires, including Ch. Cackler Of Notts and Meersbrook Bristles.

The Smooth Fox Terrier's historic profession is fox bolting. A fox bolting dog will accompany a pack of foxhounds and "bolt" after foxes, driving them out from their hiding spots and into the line of sight of the larger dogs and men on horses. Smooth Fox Terriers with white coats were less likely to be mistaken for the fox in close combat situations, and were therefore more highly prized.

Health

The Smooth Fox Terrier generally lives 12 to 15 years, and can live as long as 19 years. The breed is genetically quite healthy. Some known health problems are deafness, luxating patellas and a variety of eye disorders such as lens luxation, distichiasis, and cataracts. Skeletal problems that can occur include Legge-Perthes disease and shoulder dislocations. Myasthenia Gravis and idiopathic epilepsy have also been reported, as well as goiter.

Grooming

The Smooth Fox Terrier is basically a low-maintenance dog in terms of grooming. Hair grows all over the entire body equally, so to have the smooth clean look areas must be scissored or clippered. For normal pet maintenance, brushing the coat, keeping the nails trimmed, and cleaning the hair out of the pads of the feet is important. Brushing teeth is also recommended, a dog's bite is very important to its health. Getting your Smooth Fox Terrier used to grooming at an early age is recommended for it will be easier for you the owner to do so throughout your dogs life. Smooth Fox Terriers are known for enjoying the attention that is brought to them while grooming.

Famous Smooth-haired Fox Terriers

- Nipper, mascot of HMV and RCA; some commercials featured him portrayed as a fox terrier, though the original one was a mixed breed.
- Snitter, protagonist from the novel *The Plague Dogs*, written by Richard Adams
- Titina, travelled with Umberto Nobile on Airship Norge and Airship Italia
- Skip, from the book *My Dog Skip* by Willie Morris, although played by a Jack Russell Terrier in the film of the same name
- Dash[1], name of seven consequent dogs (among them, six smooth fox-terriers) of Sir Aurel Stein, who accompanied him in sensational archeological expeditions to Xinjiang, Iran and other countries in the early 20th century.

See also

- Fox Terrier, for additional details on history, genetics, coat color, and so on.

External links

- Smooth Fox Terrier Association UK [2]
- American Kennel Club [3]
- American Fox Terrier Club [4]
- Smooth Fox Terrier Association of America [5]

Soft-Coated Wheaten Terrier

The **Soft-Coated Wheaten Terrier** is a breed of dog originating in Ireland. There are four coat varieties: Traditional Irish, Heavy Irish, English, and American. These dogs have a single coat which sheds very little hair, so they can be more easily tolerated by people allergic to other breeds.

History

The Wheaten was bred in Ireland to be an all-purpose farm dog whose duties would have included herding, watching and guarding livestock, and vermin hunting and killing. They are believed to be related to the Kerry Blue Terrier. Today Wheaten terriers compete in obedience, agility, and tracking, and are occasionally used in animal-assisted therapy as well.

Despite its long history, the Wheaten was not recognized as a breed in Ireland by the Irish Kennel Club until 1937. In 1943 the British Kennel Club recognized the breed as well. The first Wheatens were exported to the United States in 1946 but serious interest in the breed took years to develop. Lydia Vogel was one of the first breeders of the Wheaten Terrier in the United States. Finally, in 1973, they were recognized by the American Kennel Club. The first Wheatens imported into Australia occurred in the 70's by Anubis Kennels. Since then many more have been imported. Recent importation of Irish style dogs have improved and broadened the gene pool.

Appearance

Puppies have a dark coat of either red, brown, mahogany or white. The muzzle and ears of Wheaten puppies may be black or dark brown. The dark puppy coat gradually grows out to nearly white before maturing into a wheaten-colored coat as they get older. The color can range from wheat to white, but white coats are not considered desirable by breeders and show enthusiasts. The adult coat may contain black, white, or darker brown "guard" hairs in addition to the lighter wheaten-coloured hair. If adults ever have skin injuries the resulting hair growth will be the dark color of their puppy coat before it eventually grows out to the wheat color.

The Soft-Coated Wheaten Terrier is a medium-sized dog, which ranges on average anywhere from 17 to 19 inches and weighs about 30 to 45 pounds. The breed has a square structure and is well built. Its hair does not shed like most dogs; like human hair and Poodle hair, it keeps growing, needs regular trimming, and drops just a few hairs daily.

The Irish coat tends to be thinner and silkier than the American variety.

Health

Soft Coated Wheaten Terriers are generally a long-lived breed. They are susceptible to various heritable diseases. although are most known for two protein wasting conditions: protein-losing nephropathy (PLN), where the dog loses protein from the kidneys, and protein-losing enteropathy, where the dog loses protein from the intestines (PLE) Both PLN and PLE are fatal, though there is health testing available to determine diagnosis. Wheaten owners should check their country's advised testing protocols. These conditions have an unknown mode of inheritance but there are research programs, mainly in the United States and the United Kingdom.

Other wheaten health issues are renal dysplasia, inflammatory bowel disease, Addison's disease, and cancer. Some Wheatens can also suffer from food and environmental allergies. Potential owners of wheaten terriers should discuss health issues with the breeder before deciding to get a puppy.

Temperament

The Soft-Coated Wheaten Terrier is an energetic and playful dog. They require patience and consistent positive training. Harsh methods will often result in fear aggression. A positive, even-handed approach works best with these intelligent yet headstrong terriers. They are enthusiastic greeters and will often jump up in order to lick a person's face, commonly referred to as the "Wheaten greetin'" These dogs do best when they are exercised regularly. They are cool weather dogs and can become easily overheated in hot weather. If socialized with cats as puppies they may get along fine with them; if not, care should be taken in introducing them to cats as the breed has a very strong "prey drive" because of the Breeds vermin-hunting origin. Wheatens can get along well with other dogs if properly socialized. They are extremely friendly and loving pets. Wheatens are very protective of their families, and although they may bark an alert at strangers, they rarely get aggressive. Many Wheaten owners thus say that Wheatens make great watch dogs but poor guard dogs.

Cross breeds

Wheatens are unofficially crossbred with Standard Poodles, to create the mixed breed known as the Whoodle, and with Beagles to create those known as "Wheagles". They are also a cross with a sighthound such as a greyhound, for the purpose of breeding lurchers.

External links

- Kennel Club Breed Standard [1]

Staffordshire Bull Terrier

The **Staffordshire Bull Terrier** (informally: **Staffie**, **Stafford**, **Staffross**, **Staffy** or **Staff**) is a medium-sized, short-coated, old-time breed of dog, originally bred for bull baiting.. In the early part of the twentieth century, the breed gained respectability, and it was accepted by The Kennel Club of the United Kingdom as the Staffordshire bull terrier. It is an English breed of dog related to the bull terrier and similar in appearance to the much larger American Staffordshire terrier and American pit bull terrier

Description

Appearance

The Staffordshire Bull Terrier is a medium-sized, stocky, muscular dog with athletic ability. They have a broad head, defined occipital muscles, a relatively short foreface, dark round eyes and a wide mouth with a clean scissor-like bite (the top incisors slightly overlap the bottom incisors). The ears are small. The cheek muscles are very pronounced. Their lips show no looseness, and they rarely drool. From above, the head loosely resembles a triangle. The head tapers down to a strong well-muscled neck and shoulders placed on squarely spaced forelimbs. They are tucked up in their loins and the last 1-2 ribs of their ribcage are usually visible. Their tail resembles an old fashioned pump handle. Their hind quarters are well-muscled and are what give the Staffy drive when baiting.

They are coloured brindle, black, red, fawn, blue, white, or any blending of these colors with white. White with any color over an eye is known as piebald or *pied*. Skewbald is white with fawn patches. Liver-colored and black and tan dogs sometimes occur. The coat is smooth and clings tightly to the body giving the dog a streamlined appearance.

The dogs stand at the withers and weigh (male dogs are normally up to 6 lb heavier).

The 'Staffordshire Bull Terrier' can suffer from health problems common to other dog breeds such as cataracts, hip dysplasia and breathing problems but are overall a very healthy breed.

Temperament

Although individual differences in personality exist, common traits exist throughout the Staffords. Due to its breeding, the modern dog is known for its character of indomitable courage, high intelligence, and tenacity. This, coupled with its affection for its friends (and children in particular), its off-duty quietness and trustworthy stability, make it a foremost all-purpose dog . It has been said that "No breed is more loving with its family" Because of their affinity for children, Staffordshire Bull Terriers are sometimes known as "Nanny Dogs" in England.

The breed is naturally muscular and may appear intimidating; however, because of their natural fondness for people, most Staffords are temperamentally ill-suited for guard or attack-dog training.

Staffordshire Bull Terrier puppies are very easy to house train.

Courage

The most important characteristic of all the ancestors of the Stafford was their great courage. Aggression was necessary in a fighting dog - but, whereas a dog can be trained and conditioned to be aggressive, nothing can teach him courage. This is bred in him at birth. Breeders today value the courage of their dogs. Nobody is proud to own a timid Stafford, but no sensible breeder encourages aggression towards other animals. Responsible owners and breeders deliberately avoid confrontational experiences.

Courage is important in a pet dog because more dogs bite out of fear than for any other reason. A dog who is not alarmed can cope much better with the rough and tumble of a busy family home, one of the reasons the Stafford is such a success as a dog for children. He is as hardy and fun-loving, and fearless, as they are.

Press on Bad Behaviour

Since the UK Dangerous Dogs Act made it illegal to own breeds such as the pit bull terrier, the press have reported many cases of attacks by Staffordshire Bull Terriers or dogs described as a 'Staffordshire bull terrier cross' on children, adults and family pets. The RSPCA fears that breeders are re-naming pit bulls as Staffordshire bull terriers to avoid prosecution. Also, the description 'Staffordshire terrier cross' is frequently a euphemism for a dog such as the American Pit Bull Terrier. However, the Staffordshire bull terrier, like all dog breeds, is capable of dangerous behavior. A New South Wales state government report analysing 793 dog attacks in late 2009 identified the Staffordshire bull terrier as the leading breed of dog responsible for biting humans (ahead of the Australian Cattle Dog, German Shepherd and Jack Russell Terrier). "Staffordshire" type dogs topped a similar NSW government report in 2006. However, while the report identified 279 of the 2325 total recorded attacks as by "Staffordshire" dogs, only 1 of those 2325 reported attacks was positively identified by the report as by an "English Staffordshire" (A.K.A. Staffordshire Bull Terrier). In contrast, 58 of those attacks were positively identified as by an "American Staffordshire," a uniquely different breed that is about 1/3 larger than the Staffordshire Bull Terrier.

There were 1,122 dog attack incidents reported by all New South Wales councils from 1 January 2010 to 31 March 2010. This number included harassement and bites by dogs on people and animals. The Staffordshire Bull Terrier was responsible for the largest number of attacks.

Affinity with people

Staffordshire Bull Terriers are large-hearted and usually affectionate towards humans. They express their affection through jumping up, nuzzling and pawing, and even when trained can still be 'fussy' with owners and others. Staffordshires are perhaps not suitable pets for those who prefer quiet, reserved dogs. Staffordshires are notably adaptable in terms of changing home or even owners, and unfortunately this can make them easy prey for dognappers.

RSPCA chief vet Mark Evans said: "Staffies have had a terrible press, but this is not of their own making - in fact they're wonderful dogs. If people think that Staffies have problems, they're looking at the wrong end of the dog lead! When well cared for and properly trained they can make brilliant companions. Our experience suggests that problems occur when bad owners exploit the Staffie's desire to please by training them to show aggression." .

Breed-specific legislation

The Staffordshire Bull Terrier is often subject to breed bans worldwide that target the Bull and Terrier family. However, Australia, England, and New Zealand make clear a distinction between the American Pit Bull Terrier and Staffordshire Bull Terrier and thus are exempted from Breed Specific Legislation.

History

Before the nineteenth century, bloodsports such as bull baiting, bear baiting and cock fighting were common. Bulls brought to market were set upon by dogs as a way of tenderizing the meat and providing entertainment for the spectators; and dog fights with bears, bulls and other animals were often organized as entertainment for both royalty and commoners. Early Bull and Terriers were not bred for the handsome visual specimen of today, rather they were bred for the characteristic known as gameness. The pitting of dogs against bear or bull tested the gameness, strength and skill of the dog. These early "proto-staffords" provided the ancestral foundation stock for the Staffordshire Bull Terrier, the Bull Terrier, the American Pit Bull Terrier and American Staffordshire Terrier. This common ancestor was known as the "Bull and Terrier".

These bloodsports were officially eliminated in 1835 as Britain began to introduce animal welfare laws. Since dogfights were cheaper to organize and far easier to conceal from the law than bull or bear baits, bloodsport proponents turned to pitting their dogs against each other instead. Dog fighting was used as both a bloodsport (often involving gambling) and a way to continue to test the quality of their stock. For decades afterward, dog fighting clandestinely took place in pockets of working-class Britain and America. Dogs were released into a pit, and the last dog still fighting (or occasionally, the last dog surviving) was recognized as the winner. The quality of pluckiness or "gameness" was still highly prized, and dogs that gave up during a fight were reviled as "curs".

Breeding

Kennel clubs

The breed attained UK [Kennel Club] recognition on 25 May 1935.The Staffordshire Bull Terrier Club was formed in June 1935, a couple of months after the breed was recognised by the kennel club. It is unusual for a breed to be recognised without a club in existence first, and even more unusual for their not to have been a breed standard in place! A standard was not drawn up until June 1935 at the Old Cross Guns, a Black country pub in Cradley Heath in the west Midlands. A group of 30 Stafford enthusiasts gathered there and devised the standard, as well as electing the clubs first secretary, Joseph Dunn, a well known figure in the breed. Challenge certificates were awarded to the breed in 1938, and the first champions were Ch. Gentleman Jim (bred by Joseph Dunn) and Ch. lady Eve (owned by Joseph Dunn), both taking their titles in 1939.

American

Staffordshires were imported into the US during this time. Though very popular in the United Kingdom, the Staffordshire Bull Terrier has not gained the same fame in the United States.

The American Staffordshire Terrier is not a breed for novice owners. Although it achieved American Kennel Club(AKC) registration and recognition in 1936, it had been developed since the early 1800s as a result of crosses between the bulldogs of that time and game terriers. One of the early and extremely prominent AKC registered Staffs was" Pete the Pup", dog star of the original Our Gang comedies of the 1930s.

In the US many were imported by pit fighters and used in their breeding programs to produce the American Pit Bull Terrier and American Staffordshire Terrier. Many were imported by British nationals who brought their dogs with them or U.S. expatriates who fell in love with the breed in England and brought it home. The Staffordshire breed was recognized in the U.S. in 1975.

Common Health Problems

As with any breed, irresponsible breeding can cause the spread of hereditary genetic flaws. Tests are performed to screen for these conditions.

Two of the conditions that can be detected by DNA testing are L-2-hydroxyglutaric aciduria (L2HGA) and Hereditary Cataracts (HC). This testing need only be done once. There are another two conditions which can be checked by way of an ocular examination throughout the life of a breeding stud or brood-bitch to minimize the transfer & spread of these conditions. The first is distachiasis (commonly known as "double eyelash") where eyelashes are misdirected and begin to rub against the eye, particularly the cornea, causing ocular surface damage. The second is Persistent Hyperplastic Primary Vitreous (or PHPV) which is a condition whereby the blood supply to the ocular lens fails to regress and fibrovascular tissue forms causing hazy vision.

The breed is known to be at risk from mastocytoma (mast cell tumours), often seen in the stomach area as Staffies love to sunbathe on their backs.

Puppies should be wormed at two to three weeks and no later. There are simple, liquid forms of wormer that are easy to give at this early age. The pups will need to be wormed at least twice more before they go to their new homes at around eight weeks of age. Always weigh the puppies and follow the instructions exactly.

See also

- American Staffordshire Terrier
- American Pit Bull Terrier
- American Bully
- Pit Bull
- Breed-specific legislation
- Blue Paul Terrier
- Rat-baiting
- Jock of the Bushveld

External links

- Forum for Staffordshire Bull terrier lovers (French) [1]
- [2]
- [3]
- Staffordshire Bull Terrier Italian Club (Italian) [4]

Welsh Terrier

The **Welsh Terrier** is a breed of dog, one of many British terrier breeds. It was originally bred for hunting fox, rodents and badger, but during the last century it has mainly been bred for showing. Despite this, it has retained its terrier strength of character and so requires firm, non-aggressive handling. The Welsh Terrier originates from Wales and has been claimed to be the oldest existing dog breed in the UK according to the research of Julian Calder and Alastair Bruce for their book, 'The Oldest - in celebration of Britain's living history'. The Welsh Terrier was a latecomer to the British show-ring (being primarily a working dog) and was not officially registered until the 1800s. It is currently on the UK Kennel Clubs list of breeds that are in danger of dying out, having as few as 300 or so pups registered annually, compared to the nations most popular breeds that are registered in their tens of thousands each year.

Description

Appearance

The Welsh Terrier is colored tan on the head, legs and underbelly while having a black or sometimes grizzle saddle. The breed is a sturdy and compact dog of about medium size that can grow up to 15.5 in. (39.5 cm) with a weight of 20-22 lbs (9–10 kg). The tail is usually docked and is more preferred in order to complete the image of a square dog that is as tall as it is long. The body shape is rectangular, with elongated, "brick-like" face. This shape is formed by the whiskers and beard. The hair contains two layers, an undercoat that insulates and an abrasive fur on top that protects against dirt, rain, and wind. Welsh Terriers are born mostly all black and during the first year they change the color to standard black and tan grizzle.

This breed does not shed (see Moult).

An undocked Welsh Terrier tail is only an inch or so longer than a docked tail and does not make a great deal of difference to the overall appearance. The coat does not moult out but old hairs will eventually be stripped out through play and movement etc if the coat is not regularly raked. Ungroomed coats can also fade and thin out as the old hair loses colour and texture. to keep a moult free house and a good coat on your Welsh Terrier it is necessary to rake out the coat on a regular basis. Welsh terriers need some grooming. Their fur grows a little long.

Generally speaking, the Welsh Terrier looks quite a bit like a compact Airedale Terrier.

Temperament

The Welsh Terrier has a typical terrier temperament. In the right hands, it is a happy, lively, and seldom shy or timid dog, but sometimes can have an attitude. Dogs of this breed can be devoted friends and can function either as city dogs or as country dogs.

Welsh Terriers were developed to hunt independently and this required that they be very assertive and stoic dogs. As a consequence, developing obedience in a Welsh Terrier is a long term proposition and one has to constantly work on and reinforce the training.

A Welsh Terrier is full of energy and requires regular exercise. A run around the yard during the day is insufficient. They become yappy, and if bored, they may explore and potentially cause mischief and damage. Welsh Terriers need a challenge to keep them entertained. For example, they love chasing toys and love swimming (a good example would be lake activities with their families).

Welsh Terriers get along well with children; they love to play and follow a child as it plays, however, they will often tug at pant legs and can knock young ones off their feet. If they are around young children at an early age, they will easily learn to play more gently.

As with all breeds, it is important to socialize Welsh Terriers as early as possible to a wide range of dogs, people, and experiences.

Health

The body of the Welsh Terrier is normal and healthy so that the physique is durable and lasting. Some studies have suggested a genetic predisposition to Glaucoma, as yet inconclusive . A healthy Welsh Terrier lives around 12 to 13 years on average and stays active and alert up to a high age if it is well taken care of and healthy.

Notable Welsh Terriers

- Charlie, pet of John F. Kennedy
- Clement Attlee, Ist Earl Attlee, Prime Minister of the United Kingdom 1945-1951 owned a Welsh Terrier. The dog is incorporated in to Earl Attlee's coat-of-arms
- Gwen, Welsh Terrier pet of Edward, Prince of Wales, later King Edward VIII.

References

- College of Veterinary Medicine, University of Missouri [1]

External links

- Welsh Terriers and Friends - British-based site about the breed [2]
- The Welsh Terrier Association [3]
- The Welsh Terrier Club of America [4]

West Highland White Terrier

West Highland White Terriers, commonly known as **Westies**, are a breed of dog known for their distinctive white coat. Originating in Scotland, the breed was used to seek and dig out foxes and badgers. This breed is commonly recognized through its use as a mascot for Black & White (a brand of Scotch whisky), Cesar brand dog food, and various other logos.

Appearance

Commonly, Westies have bright, deep-set eyes that are dark in color. Their ears are small, pointed, and erect. A male typically weighs between and a female between . average height is at the withers. The Kennel Club has recommended that their tails, typically "carrot-shaped", should never be docked; hence the tail should be between .

They also have deep chests, muscular limbs, a huge skull, a large black nose, a short and a closely fitted jaw with "scissors" bite (lower canines locked in front of upper canines, upper incisors locked over lower incisors). Their teeth generally appear quite large for the size of the dog. Westies have a very strong bone structure for their size.

They have a soft, dense, thick undercoat and a rough outer coat, about 2 inches long, that requires regular grooming. Some Westies have "wheaten tippings" on their backs, though for individuals put forward for conformation showing this can be regarded as undesirable. Also, some Westies do not have a top coarse coat, and just a second silky coat.

This breed is a non-shedding dog. As they develop into adults, their thinner "puppy coat" is normally removed by either 'hand-stripping' or otherwise clipping.

Care

Westies are prone to allergies and dry skin problems, and bathing too frequently may aggravate these problems. Washing once a month or on a longer interval will generally not cause problems. However, frequent brushings are needed to keep the coat clean and oils evenly distributed throughout the coat. Washing with a detergent-free, baby-oriented, or another soft skin shampoo will help keep a Westie's skin hydrated. Weekly washing of the inside of the ears with cotton balls will prevent oil and wax build-up and ear infections. Water in the ears must be removed before an infection develops. Westies should be groomed at least every 6 weeks, and bathed and brushed as needed between appointments.

Westies love dog treats which can be helpful for dogs to have positive habits. Westie particularly love dog treats made from beef, chicken, lamb and rice such as Bully Sticks, Greenies, Dog Beef Jerky, Chicken Dog Treats, Lamb Treats...etc. Westies are very sensitive, so make sure to give the right dog treats. Dog treats for Westies should always be the "big" ones so that it takes a long time to get a small piece in their mouth. A Westie can get small pieces stuck in their throat and the raw hide can wear a hole through the esophagus. The chews become soft and can also get stuck in the roof of the mouth. Dog treats such as pig ears and raw hides are not good for Westies. Wesites are generally behaved around children, however, they can become restless when excited.

Health

As with most other dogs, Westies generally require around thirteen hours of sleep per day. In order to acquire their needed sleep, Westies will usually follow the sleep patterns of their human companions and also take several naps during the day. The average lifespan of a Westie can range from 12 to 17 years. They also need regular walking, although if they have access to a large yard they can exercise on their own.

Craniomandibular osteopathy

Westie puppies may be affected by craniomandibular osteopathy, a disease also known "lion jaw". (The disease is an autosomal recessive condition and so a puppy can only be affected by it if both its parents are carriers of the faulty gene.) With this disease, the only current way to identify carrier breeding stock is if an affected puppy is produced. Therefore, breeders may be unaware that breeding stock are carriers until an affected puppy is born. Craniomandibular osteopathy is a non-neoplastic proliferative disease of the ventral mandibular ramus, occipital base of the skull and tympanic bullae, characterised by excessive bone deposition in these areas. In most incidences, the defect is bilateral, although this is not always the case. The disease varies in severity, the region(s) affected and the individual pain threshold of the affected puppy. Definitive diagnosis is achieved by radiographic examination.

Craniomandibular osteopathy is extremely painful to the puppy. Affected puppies will most likely display signs of pain or discomfort, such as yelping, when their head is touched and when chewing or eating. The puppy may be lethargic and be reluctant to eat as a result.

The condition usually manifests when the puppy is around 3–6 months of age, and regresses spontaneously around 12 months of age. Treatment of the disease is concerned with managing the symptoms and providing appropriate analgesia to improve quality of life and enable the puppy to eat until the disease resolves spontaneously. Corticosteroids are the usual therapeutic agents used to manage the disease. The exact treatment protocol depends on the severity, localisation and pain sensitivity of the affected puppy. In extreme cases, euthanasia may be required.

History

The breed was originally named the Poltalloch terrier, after the estate in the Argyll region of western Scotland where they were developed by Colonel Edward Donald Malcolm (1837–1930) and his family. It is said that the breed gained its white coat after the Colonel's red terrier was mistaken for a fox and shot: the dog was to be white in colour so as to help distinguish it from its quarry. The Westie came to the United States in the early 1900s, originally called Roseneath Terrior. The name was changed to reflect the breed's origins more clearly. Some dog breeders and fanciers also believe that Westies developed with contributions from white dogs in the litters of Cairn Terriers. Others believe that there are contributions from similar dogs developed by the 8th Duke of Argyll (Chieftain of Clan Campbell).

In popular culture

- Author John Green owns a West Highland Terrier named Fireball Wilson Roberts.
- Fictional police officer Hamish Macbeth owns a West Highland Terrier named Wee Jock.
- On the medical drama "House" on episode *Family*, House (Hugh Laurie) must babysit Wilson's ex-wife's dog, Hector. Though House appears to dislike Hector at first, the two form a unique bond as Hector gnaws on House's cane, ransacks his apartment, and eats his pills. The end of the episode reveals Hector imitating House's limp.
- Similarly, Bertie Wooster (also played by Hugh Laurie) must frequently babysit his Aunt Agatha's dog, MacIntosh, played by a West Highland White Terrier (although its breed is given as an Aberdeen Terrier), in the television series Jeeves and Wooster.
- Actor Robert Pattinson, from the Twilight, The Twilight Saga: New Moon, and Remember Me, owns a West Highland white Terrier named Patty.

In advertising

- A West Highland White Terrier is used as the mascot for Cesar Dog food.
- The logo for London fashion brand Radley is a cartoon Westie.
- The clothing brand Juicy Couture often features multicolored Westies in their advertisements.
- In the animated sitcom King of the Hill, the Souphanousinphones own a Westie named Doggie Khan.

- A Westie is the Mascot for Scotch Fur Fighter Hair Remover products

References

- Buckley, Holland (1911), *The West Highland White Terrier,* Illustrated Kennel News Co., ISBN 0765108119
- Cleland, Sheila (1995), *Pet Owner's Guide to the West Highland White Terrier,* Ringpress Books Ltd., ISBN 1860540155
- Wallace, Martin (1996), *Guide to Owning a West Highland White Terrier,* TFH Publications, ISBN 0793818656
- Weiss, Seymour N. (1996), *The West Highland White Terrier: An Owner's Guide to a Happy Healthy Pet,* Howell Book House Inc., ISBN 0876054947
- *West Highland White Terrier*, Penelope Ruggles-Smythe (Interpret Publishing 1999), ISBN 1902389123.
- *West Highland White Terrier: An Owner's Guide*, Robert Killick (Collins 2003), ISBN 000717831X.

Wire Fox Terrier

The **Wire Fox Terrier** is a breed of dog, one of many terrier breeds. It is an instantly recognizable fox terrier breed. Although it bears a resemblance to the Smooth Fox Terrier, they are believed to have been developed separately.

Appearance

The wire fox terrier is a sturdy, balanced dog weighing between 7 and 9.5 kg (15 and 21 lb). Its rough, broken coat is distinctive. Coat color consists of a predominant white base with brown markings of the face and ears, and usually a black saddle or large splotch of color; there may be other black or brown markings on the body. The wire in the photo at left sports the traditional white, black and buff tri-color coat. The wire in the upper right hand photo appears to be a ginger, a wire without black markings.

Temperament

Two of the Wire Fox Terriers' most distinctive traits are their enormous amount of energy and intelligence. They have a low threshold for boredom and require stimulation, exercise and attention. Indeed, once ingrained in the family, they are an inquisitive pet. Always with a nosey for your business and especially comfort time on the couch or bed in the evening, the wirefox is a true companion animal. Most truly love water and are apt for a swim. A life jacket is recommended. The Wire Fox

Terrier should be alert, quick, and ready to respond accordingly while being keen of expression and friendly and forthcoming. They can be very loving and exceedingly playful if they receive the proper care. They are bred to be independent thinkers, capable of tactical maneuvering for vermin and other sport. Their high level of intelligence makes them a dog that is not suited for everyone. Wire Hair Fox Terriers are hand stripped; if the hair becomes too long, their hair should be taken out by hand (for show purposes). Many Wire Fox pets are clipped 3 - 4 times a year by a groomer. Clipping dulls the colors but is acceptable and quite comfortable for pet quality dogs.

History

The wire fox terrier was developed in England by fox hunting enthusiasts and is believed descended from a now-extinct rough-coated, black-and-tan working terrier of Wales, Derbyshire, and Durham. The breed was also believed to have been bred to chase foxes into their burrows underground, and their short, strong, usually docked, tails were used as handles by the hunter to pull them back out.

Although it is said Queen Victoria owned one, and her son and heir, King Edward VII of Great Britain did own the wire fox terrier, Caesar, the wire fox terrier was not popular as a family pet until the 1930s, when *The Thin Man* series of feature films was created. Asta, the canine member of the Charles family, was a Wire-Haired Fox Terrier, and the popularity of the breed soared. Milou (Snowy) from *The Adventures of Tintin* comic strip is also a Wire Fox Terrier.

In the late 20th century, the popularity of the breed declined again, most likely due to changing living conditions in the Western world and the difficulty of keeping hunting terriers in cities due to their strong prey instincts.

The wire fox terrier has the distinction of having received more Best in Show titles at major conformation shows than any other breed. Wire fox terriers kept as pets show the loyalty, intelligence, independence, playfulness and breeding befitting such a storied breed.

Ch. Matford Vic, a Wire Fox Terrier, is one of only five dogs to have won the Westminster Kennel Club Dog Show on more than one occasion. He won the competition twice, in 1915 and 1916. The only dog to win it on more occasions was Ch. Warren Remedy, a Smooth Fox Terrier, who won it on three occasions between 1907 and 1909.

Noteworthy Wire Fox Terriers

- Archie, owned by Gill Raddings Stunt Dogs starred in ITV's Catwalk Dogs.
- Asta, from *The Thin Man films adaptation* (the novel's breed was a Schnauzer)
- Bob, from the *Hercule Poirot* episode *Dumb Witness*
- Bunny, from *Hudson Hawk*
- Caesar, the companion of King Edward VII of the United Kingdom
- Charles, brought to Ceylon by Leonard Woolf in 1905
- Chester, in the film Jack Frost
- Dášeňka, the dog of Czechoslovak writer and journalist Karel Čapek - also featured as main hero of "Dášeňka čili život štěněte" book.
- George, from *Bringing Up Baby*
- Ike Larue, from the *Ike Larue* series, written and illustrated by Mark Teague
- Moll, from the book "Memoirs of a Fox Hunting Man"
- Mr. Smith, from *The Awful Truth*
- Nellie, inspiration for *Nellie the Lighthouse Dog* (Nellie was formerly known as Hockney) by Jane Scarpino; Nellie's owner, Robert Ensor, illustrated
- Pan, the companion of A.L. Westgard, AAA pathfinder. Pan was the mascot of the dedication tour for the National Park to Park Highway in 1920.
- Polly, a white rough terrier companion to Charles Darwin
- Scruffy, the Muirs' Wire Fox Terrier on The Ghost and Mrs. Muir
- Skippy, from *Topper Takes a Trip*
- Snowy (*French: Milou*), companion of Tintin
- "The dog," from the Selchow and Righter board game "Mr. Doodle's Dog"
- Wessex, the wire of British novelist ("Tess of the d'Ubervilles")Thomas Hardy
- Willy, from *Ask the Dust*
- Wuffles, the Patrician's dog in the *Discworld* Series

Asta, George, Mr. Smith and Skippy were all played by the canine actor, Skippy.

Grooming Wire Fox Terriers have to be groomed using a special technique called hand stripping. You can do this by going to a groomer near you and asking if they do hand stripping, which most grooming facilities do.

See also

- Fox Terrier, for additional details on history, genetics, coat color, and so on.

External links

- The Wire Fox Terrier Association [1]
- American Fox Terrier Club, Inc. [2]

Article Sources and Contributors

Breed Groups (dog) *Source*: http://en.wikipedia.org/?oldid=371298317 *Contributors*: 1 anonymous edits

American Kennel Club *Source*: http://en.wikipedia.org/?oldid=373448194 *Contributors*: 07bargem

Terrier Group *Source*: http://en.wikipedia.org/?oldid=367873723 *Contributors*:

Airedale Terrier *Source*: http://en.wikipedia.org/?oldid=376200200 *Contributors*:

American Staffordshire Terrier *Source*: http://en.wikipedia.org/?oldid=371048709 *Contributors*: 1 anonymous edits

Australian Terrier *Source*: http://en.wikipedia.org/?oldid=375359395 *Contributors*: Chuck in MA

Bedlington Terrier *Source*: http://en.wikipedia.org/?oldid=376115160 *Contributors*: 1 anonymous edits

Border Terrier *Source*: http://en.wikipedia.org/?oldid=367019365 *Contributors*: 1 anonymous edits

Bull Terrier *Source*: http://en.wikipedia.org/?oldid=376340833 *Contributors*: Boing! said Zebedee

Cairn Terrier *Source*: http://en.wikipedia.org/?oldid=376164037 *Contributors*:

Dandie Dinmont Terrier *Source*: http://en.wikipedia.org/?oldid=375075996 *Contributors*: Thumperward

Glen of Imaal Terrier *Source*: http://en.wikipedia.org/?oldid=371593257 *Contributors*:

Irish Terrier *Source*: http://en.wikipedia.org/?oldid=367179404 *Contributors*:

Kerry Blue Terrier *Source*: http://en.wikipedia.org/?oldid=375763694 *Contributors*: 1 anonymous edits

Lakeland Terrier *Source*: http://en.wikipedia.org/?oldid=368119984 *Contributors*: Auntof6

Manchester Terrier *Source*: http://en.wikipedia.org/?oldid=372456210 *Contributors*: Chowbok

Bull Terrier (Miniature) *Source*: http://en.wikipedia.org/?oldid=374311298 *Contributors*: 1 anonymous edits

Miniature Schnauzer *Source*: http://en.wikipedia.org/?oldid=376648966 *Contributors*: Athlem

Norfolk Terrier *Source*: http://en.wikipedia.org/?oldid=373127310 *Contributors*: Jeffnesbitt

Norwich Terrier *Source*: http://en.wikipedia.org/?oldid=376129525 *Contributors*: Tmslone

Parson Russell Terrier *Source*: http://en.wikipedia.org/?oldid=374945733 *Contributors*: The Blade of the Northern Lights

Scottish Terrier *Source*: http://en.wikipedia.org/?oldid=376272682 *Contributors*: Ohnoitsjamie

Sealyham Terrier *Source*: http://en.wikipedia.org/?oldid=365055187 *Contributors*:

Skye Terrier *Source*: http://en.wikipedia.org/?oldid=374201927 *Contributors*: Kelvin Samuel

Fox Terrier (Smooth) *Source*: http://en.wikipedia.org/?oldid=368771461 *Contributors*: Mercy

Soft-Coated Wheaten Terrier *Source*: http://en.wikipedia.org/?oldid=373285939 *Contributors*: Notedgrant

Staffordshire Bull Terrier *Source*: http://en.wikipedia.org/?oldid=376046556 *Contributors*: Oosh

Welsh Terrier *Source*: http://en.wikipedia.org/?oldid=366367759 *Contributors*:

West Highland White Terrier *Source*: http://en.wikipedia.org/?oldid=375211464 *Contributors*: 1 anonymous edits

Wire Fox Terrier *Source*: http://en.wikipedia.org/?oldid=373385317 *Contributors*: 1 anonymous edits

LaVergne, TN USA
14 December 2010
208751LV00009B/26/P

10